Ninety Biblical Story Lessons for Adults

Ninety Biblical Story Lessons for Adults

Models for Biblical Storytelling

Jim Roché

WIPF & STOCK · Eugene, Oregon

NINETY BIBLICAL STORY LESSONS FOR ADULTS
Models for Biblical Storytelling

Copyright © 2024 Jim Roché. All rights reserved. Except for brief quotations in critical publications or reviews, no part of this book may be reproduced in any manner without prior written permission from the publisher. Write: Permissions, Wipf and Stock Publishers, 199 W. 8th Ave., Suite 3, Eugene, OR 97401.

Wipf & Stock
An Imprint of Wipf and Stock Publishers
199 W. 8th Ave., Suite 3
Eugene, OR 97401

www.wipfandstock.com

PAPERBACK ISBN: 979-8-3852-0718-3
HARDCOVER ISBN: 979-8-3852-0719-0
EBOOK ISBN: 979-8-3852-0720-6

VERSION NUMBER 02/29/24

Contents

Acknowledgments | ix

Introduction | 1
    How to Use This Book | 2
    How Not to Use This Book | 4

Chapter 1: Creating an Oral Story Lesson | 7
    The Story Lesson Format | 10
    The Story Selection Process | 16

Chapter 2: Thirty Old Testament Story Lessons | 29
    OT 1: God Created a Pure and Perfect Universe | 30
    OT 2: Questioning God's Goodness Brought Sin | 32
    OT 3: Cain's Jealousy Resulted in Abel's Murder | 34
    OT 4: God Flooded Earth but Rescued Noah | 36
    OT 5: Abram Called by God to Make a Nation | 38
    OT 6: Abram Tested God's Promises to Him | 40
    OT 7: Sarah Died and Isaac Prepared to Lead | 42
    OT 8: Abraham's Family Lacked Integrity | 44
    OT 9: Joseph Trusted despite Being Imprisoned | 46
    OT 10: Moses Led the Exodus from Egypt | 48
    OT 11: God Provided for Israel's Needs | 50
    OT 12: Aaron and Miriam Dishonored Moses | 52
    OT 13: Israel Dishonored God at Mount Sinai | 54
    OT 14: God Established the Sacrificial System | 56
    OT 15: The Spies Refused God's Promised Land | 58
    OT 16: Rahab Believed God's Promise at Jericho | 60
    OT 17: The Israelites Were Defeated at Ai | 62

OT 18: Israel Was Deceived before Defeating Kings | 64
OT 19: Reluctant Gideon Defeated the Midianites | 66
OT 20: Israel Rejected God and Asked for a King | 68
OT 21: God Rejected Saul as King | 70
OT 22: David Anointed as King | 72
OT 23: David's Unfaithfulness and Discipline | 74
OT 24: Solomon Ruled with Wisdom but Failed | 76
OT 25: Israel Divided into Two Kingdoms | 78
OT 26: Prophet Elijah Fought Wicked King Ahab | 80
OT 27: God Delayed Assyria's Discipline of Judah | 82
OT 28: The Judeans Were Exiled to Babylon | 84
OT 29: Kings Allowed Judah's Return to Rebuild | 86
OT 30: God Promised Future Goodness to Israel | 88

Chapter 3: Thirty Story Lessons from the Life of Jesus | 91

J 1: Announcement of Jesus's Birth | 92
J 2: Jesus Changed Water to Wine | 94
J 3: Jesus Recruited His Disciples | 96
J 4: Jesus Fed Five Thousand Who Heard Him | 98
J 5: Jesus Walked on Water | 100
J 6: Jesus Stopped a Storm at Sea | 102
J 7: Jesus Healed from a Distance | 104
J 8: Jesus Healed a Man Born Blind | 106
J 9: Jesus Raised the Widow's Son from the Dead | 108
J 10: Jesus Raised Jairus's Daughter from the Dead | 110
J 11: Jesus Raised Lazarus from the Dead | 112
J 12: Jesus Taught to Love Enemies | 114
J 13: Jesus Taught to Love Strangers | 116
J 14: Jesus Taught Personal Righteousness | 118
J 15: Jesus Taught against Self-Righteousness | 120
J 16: Jesus Taught about Greed and Worry | 122
J 17: Jesus Taught Samaritan about Worship | 124
J 18: Jesus Taught about Father and Sons | 126
J 19: Jesus Is the Good Shepherd | 128
J 20: Jesus Is the Good Leader | 130
J 21: Jesus Forgave Sins as He Healed a Paralytic | 132
J 22: Jesus Defended Healing on the Sabbath | 134
J 23: Jesus Challenged Religious Practices | 136
J 24: Jesus Criticized Because of His Friends | 138

J 25: Religious Leaders Tried to Trap Jesus | 140
J 26: Jesus Arrested and Stood for Trial | 142
J 27: Jesus Tortured, Crucified, and Killed | 144
J 28: Confirmation of Jesus's Death and Burial | 146
J 29: Jesus Resurrected from Burial Tomb | 148
J 30: Jesus Ascended to Heaven | 150

Chapter 4: Thirty New Testament Story Lessons | 153

NT 1: The Holy Spirit Arrived on Pentecost | 154
NT 2: A Lame Man Was Healed in the Name of Jesus | 156
NT 3: Man and Wife Lied to the Holy Spirit | 158
NT 4: Jews Persecuted Stephen to His Death | 160
NT 5: Saul, a Persecutor, Converted by Jesus | 162
NT 6: Saul's Conversion Met with Disbelief | 164
NT 7: Phillip Led by the Spirit to an Ethiopian | 166
NT 8: Peter Led by the Spirit to Roman Gentiles | 168
NT 9: Peter Led by the Spirit Out of a Prison | 170
NT 10: Persecution Scattered the Jerusalem Believers | 172
NT 11: Persecution Directed Paul to Other Cities | 174
NT 12: Church Recognized Salvation by Grace | 176
NT 13: Paul and Silas Freed by an Earthquake | 178
NT 14: Paul Debated Greek Philosophy in Athens | 180
NT 15: Paul Addressed Church Disunity in Corinth | 182
NT 16: Paul Taught Faith to Jew and Gentile in Rome | 184
NT 17: Paul Affirmed Jesus's Resurrection | 186
NT 18: Paul Taught Unity by Grace in Ephesus | 188
NT 19: Paul's Imitators Had No Spiritual Authority | 190
NT 20: Paul Rejected Using Jewish Law to Mature | 192
NT 21: Paul Used Persecution to Glorify God | 194
NT 22: Favoritism Breaks God's Law of Love | 196
NT 23: Hope Overcomes Shame and Persecution | 198
NT 24: From Resurrection to the Kingdom | 200
NT 25: God Uses the Weak and Humble | 202
NT 26: Serving Others Using Different Gifts | 204
NT 27: The Indwelling Spirit Gives Power over Sin | 206
NT 28: God Controls All Things to Guarantee Hope | 208
NT 29: Forgiveness Restores Fellowship with God | 210
NT 30: Satan's Works and Jesus's Glory Revealed | 212

Acknowledgments

Though this author might have worked in solitude, this project could not have been completed without a team of persistent encouragers and supporters. The monthly encouragements from friends like Jeff and Judy, the infrequent but timely support of Pastor Don at COD, and the prayers of many like Nadine and Shirley were invaluable resources. Local support through prayers from our church family like Joe and Nina and our small group at my local church were similarly valuable. I was stretched and strengthened by the skill and wisdom of J. O. pouring decades of his rich storytelling experiences into me. My colleague in Spain, Norma A., provided feedback and networking connections as she advocated storytelling among her ministry friends. And above and over all of these gifts, there were the enablement, teaching, and insights gifted by the Holy Spirit, which will hopefully bring glory to God, for these are his stories; he was and remains the True Author. To all of you, my thanks.

Introduction

THE BIBLE OFFERS THE promise that God desires to have a personal relationship with the centerpiece of his creation—people! Have you ever had a personal relationship with someone that didn't begin with an introduction? The Bible records many insightful stories describing how God initiated introductions of himself to people and then built relationships with them over time.

Introductions are not relationships. They hold the potential of becoming relationships, but they are usually only short, simple, self-identifying summaries given to one another. The potential of a future relationship is dependent upon the building of trust and love in future times through shared events. But it begins with an introduction.

Similarly, the ninety stories in this book are not intended to be thorough, comprehensive Bible studies offering detailed theological or cultural insights. Instead, these ninety stories describe persons who expose their beliefs and values during their introduction with God and give us time to reflect and identify with them. We can learn from them and share these lessons with others. The story lessons in this book are structured to help new believers hear, learn, remember, and repeat these biblical encounters with God to friends, families, and communities in their own words and in common, casual settings.

Mature Christian believers can sometimes become so filled with theological details and a desire to share all they've learned that their stories become too complicated for young believers or inquirers to repeat all that information to others. These lessons are intended to be told using stories, because over two-thirds of the world's population prefer to process information they hear, see, or experience rather than through literate, printed media. Storytelling is safe, nonconfrontational, and inexpensive to reproduce.

Stories can be easily and quickly concluded if the listeners appear to be agitated by Christian stories. And best of all, storytelling does not require mature, trained teachers to share the story lesson; anyone is qualified to tell a story that potentially enables those listeners to repeat stories to others.

To equip storytellers, a story should be short, simple, easily remembered, and easily reproduced. Being "short" means it has both a clear beginning and an ending; the story cannot wander, trying to discover how it will begin or end!

Being "simple" means there are no references to other stories in the Bible (cross-references) or that the story is filled with descriptive but unnecessary words. Each story should have only one focused point leading to a discussion but not to an argument for the storyteller's personal conclusions. It's all about discussions and discoveries between the listener and the storyteller.

Being "easily remembered" means reducing the story to three or four memorable points so the story in its entirety can be recalled and retold to others by reviewing a few key lines by the storyteller.

Being "easily reproduced" reminds the story designer that the storytellers' audiences are not limited only to those listening to them, but to spiritual generations to come. This means the next listener must be able to tell the story to another generation whom the lesson designer may never meet. Being "easily reproduced" also means that the design *process* should repeat itself just as the story *content* is repeated.

This collection of ninety biblical story lessons is educationally designed to meet the learning preferences of oral learners, fulfill the mission strategy through multiplication of spiritual generations (2 Tim 2:2), and to challenge non-biblical worldviews using conceptual change teaching strategies.

How to Use This Book

Thirty story lessons are taken from the Old Testament in chronological order from creation to the return of Israel's exiles from captivity. These story lessons are numbered with an OT ("Old Testament") prefix. They are followed by thirty story lessons from the life of Jesus taken from the Gospels and numbered with a J ("Jesus") prefix. Finally, thirty story lessons are taken from the New Testament, beginning with the book of Acts through the book of Revelation, and are numbered with a NT ("New Testament") prefix.

Introduction

These ninety story lessons were selected to introduce God to listeners using biblical stories told by both mature believers *and* new believers or even inquirers. The spiritual power of these story lessons is not in the storyteller but in the stories themselves. If you accept that assertion, you can support the enlistment and expectations of new storytellers for whom the maturity of their new faith is still before them.

New believers are strategically invaluable because they are the entrance gate to their unreached friends and social communities. These new believers should not be lifted out of their current relationships to saturate them into already established Christian cultures. Rather, they need to form their new Christian culture *within* their community! These biblical stories provide examples and lessons how to grow their Christian community within their culture. How that was done in the first century is found in the stories of the New Testament. Again, the power is in the stories, not the person!

Jesus described himself as the way, the truth, and the life (John 14:6). The storyteller's role is to faithfully describe the events and interactions that reveal how Jesus's way differs from others' non-biblical ways. Telling a story provides a platform and opportunity to initiate a friendly discussion prompted by discovering how the beliefs and values of different worldviews shape the personal, political, or spiritual results of the characters. Were the results spectacularly beneficial or disastrously bad for those in the story? How could those influences and results be recognized or applied today?

Each story lesson contains educational elements as part of the lesson design that are essential to the learning process. The presentation of information, the relevance of the story to the listener, the questions to promote a dialogue between storyteller and listener, Scripture memory, and a deeply personal question should be thought through and prayerfully developed before telling the story. The story itself is only one of seven parts of the story lesson.

These stories can be told in a variety of settings. They can be used as casual conversations between friends or as a presentation before large or small groups of listeners. The best preparation for either presentation format is to first form small gatherings of at least four people who learn the stories by practicing with each other. These small gatherings of storytellers and story designers need to contextualize the story for each audience of listeners and then present the stories either sequentially or according to the immediate need of the listeners.

For potential audience opportunities, consider outreaches to refugees, immigrants, vacation Bible school programs, international students (new believers who can take the stories back to their homelands using now-familiar stories instead of "restricted" books that may be confiscated upon reentry to hostile countries). Always encourage listeners to repeat stories they've heard to their friends and thus fulfill the generational goal of 2 Tim 2:2.

How Not to Use This Book

Though the story lessons are carefully written to be short, simple, and easily repeatable, the specific words should not be memorized. When depending on memorized words, the new storyteller will often pause while trying to recall the next critical word to say. The movement of the story becomes halted and an awkward silence follows until that troublesome word is hopefully recovered so the story can continue. This is not the process we hope to see modeled for future generations. It is very helpful to memorize the first and the last sentences to get the story beginning and ending without struggling, but everything said in between should be told naturally. Particularly for those not used to recalling longer stories, it is often easier to visualize the story as a series of pictures and conversations. Then the storyteller simply recalls the scene and describes what's happening in each visualization. Among those in the movie industry, this practice is called "storyboarding" and is commonly used to visualize a new story unfolding and characters' positions and actions.

Because the objective of these stories is to have new listeners and believers retelling the story to successive spiritual generations, the storyteller is always modeling a comfortable, natural conversation so the listener can similarly casually retell each story using their own vocabulary to other oral-preference learners. Therefore, minor changes to the words by oral learners is not just permitted but encouraged—as long as the story remains accurate! That's another reason for forming small groups to practice with each other in the practice of storytelling, but also to correct one another to keep the story accurate.

The stories are written in this book to model the approximate length of the story and indicate which details are critical to include and which irrelevant details can be left out to keep the story short, simple, and focused on a single, misunderstood belief by the listener. Always design and practice the story as if being retold by spiritual great-grandchildren. This book

Introduction

is an attempt to cross the barrier from literacy to orality, trusting in the power of the Holy Spirit to honor his word and allow that "faith comes from hearing and hearing by the word of Christ" (Rom 5:17).

Chapter 1

Creating an Oral Story Lesson

THE GOAL OF BIBLICAL storytelling is not simply to communicate information but to change how a person views the world and their place in it. Everyone wants to know if their own surrounding world is either a hostile or a supportive environment for them. Everyone wants to live in good health and enjoy successful lives by understanding how the world works and conducting themselves according to the principles of the world. Where do such knowledge and ability originate?

From our earliest days, we are trained and taught how to live through our families, caregivers, and communities. We learn key concepts, gather new information, and add values and skills to interact with others who think the same way we do. With experience, we begin building a comprehensive worldview. The details of how such concepts are formed and challenged are presented in greater detail in my first book, *Biblical Storytelling Design: Understanding Why Oral Stories Work* (Wipf and Stock, 2020).

But no one who teaches these concepts—either formally or informally—possesses all understanding. We organize all the information we gather into categories of our own making but relying upon others who have formed their opinions on what should be emphasized and what should be ignored. Some perspectives are from a purely materialistic perspective and ignore spiritual perspectives. Others come from political, sociological, or economic perspectives. Though all of this, we eventually recognize that some conceptions we have chosen to believe are actually misconceptions. How does a good teacher help a good learner identify and correct their own misconceptions?

A good teaching strategy for correcting misconceptions has four steps. The first step is to get others aware of their own beliefs. So many of our beliefs are assumed and not critically questioned or expressed. These beliefs must be raised to the listeners' conscious level with the ability to communicate—even to themselves—what and why they believe.

The second step presents the same issue from a different and biblical perspective. Before designing or telling a story, Jesus already knew what the listener's faulty misconception was. That misconception becomes the story's purpose and the challenge to overcome through discovery, reflection, and evaluation by the listener. *Do not overlook this step; identifying the misconception is at the core of the story lesson!*

The third step encourages the listeners to compare and contrast the two concepts against each other: the first and familiar concept developed from a natural worldview against the second concept developed from a biblical worldview. During this comparison stage, the listeners should evaluate which concept held the better promise for hope and success in this world and appeared as authoritative and defensible truth.

The fourth step calls upon the listeners to make a decision about which perspective to accept and which perspective to reject. If the acceptance and rejection are not both clearly made, the listener is left to conclude either response is valid according to the situation. The listener must make a clearly recognized decision that will make a change. Only the listener can create and therefore change a personal worldview—not the storyteller!

These four steps were illustrated when Jesus talked with an expert of the law and designed the story known as the good Samaritan (Luke 10:25–37; story lesson J-13 in this book). An expert teacher of the law asked Jesus what he had to do to inherit eternal life. Jesus asked him what the law said, and the expert replied, "Love the Lord your God with all your heart, soul, mind, and strength and love your neighbor as yourself." Jesus commended him for his correct answer, but the expert knew he didn't fulfill that high expectation of loving his neighbor as himself, though he still wanted to prove himself justified. He relied upon a contemporary, debated argument about this verse, which shifted the attention from what the person should do (love) to questioning how the law defined a neighbor. The disputed passage about the neighbor in the law uses two different Hebrew words for "neighbor" (Lev 19:13–18). One word used "neighbor" as a friend or companion with a personal relationship, but the other word emphasized having equal social status. For example, this argument allowed the Essenes—a religious group at the time of Jesus—to qualify only other Essenes as neighbors, so they needed to love only other Essenes to fulfill the law. And the Jews generally interpreted only other Jews as their neighbors.

As the teacher left Jesus, he questioned, "But who is my neighbor?" Jesus knew the expert's interpretation was wrong and needed correction. Notice that Jesus didn't tell the expert he was wrong. Jesus didn't teach the expert and give him all the answers he needed to know. Jesus didn't rely on his own authority. Instead, Jesus designed a story for the teacher to discover the truth for himself.

Jesus set the context by saying, "A man was traveling on the road when he was beaten by robbers who left him for dead. A priest came by later and, when he saw the man, crossed to the other side of the road and continued on as did another Levite." Remember: the first step is to raise the listener's own beliefs to a conscious level. What was going through the expert teacher's mind hearing the priest and Levite crossed the road to avoid the victim? He wouldn't have thought anything was unusual with their actions—he would have done the very same thing. But Jesus caused the teacher to raise his beliefs to a conscious level.

The second step required replaying the story from a different, biblical perspective. Jesus used a Samaritan as the biblical perspective. Certainly, using a Samaritan eliminated either definition of neighbor (equal status or personal relationship) as relevant to the story. Instead, the Samaritan treated and cared for the victim at personal cost. Jesus asked the teacher to compare the two perspectives as to which response would be better (step 3). The expert teacher evaluated the responses and concluded a different criterion defined loving a neighbor; it was compassion. Jesus didn't tell him it should be "compassion." Instead, compassion was the expert teacher's own choice for defining a neighbor; it was his discovery. With that, Jesus brought the expert to a firm conclusion on his discovery and commanded, "Go and do the same" (step 4). No lecture; just a story with a four-step process that relied upon the listener's self-discovery to edit his personal worldview and change his belief about who his neighbor was. I suggest the teacher of the law was so impacted by the lesson that he would tell the story to anyone in the future who had a question about loving someone's neighbor.

Ninety Biblical Story Lessons for Adults

The Story Lesson Format

Every one of the ninety story lessons is built using the same design. Faithfully following the design process guides the story designer/creator through the same design steps to create a new story lesson. The consistent presentation and discussion of a story lesson makes the presentation itself become familiar and protects the storyteller from accidentally missing critical additional information that should be included in the story. The story design should always include the following design elements:

1. Misconceptions
2. Passage
3. Main Parts
4. Story
5. Questions
6. Scripture Memory
7. Hook Question

A story designer must use all seven steps to create a story lesson, but a story teller should not share the misconceptions (part 1) with the listener. Instead, the misconceptions should be discovered by the listeners. Identifying the passage (part 2) is optional if the Bible—as the story source—may generate a negative reaction. But the passage may be necessary to use later for becoming authoritative and provide verification for the listener.

Specifically identifying the main parts of the story (part 3) is not for the listener's benefit and therefore not shared as a part of the lesson. It is, however, an aid to the storyteller to remember the key story parts and ensure the progressive movement of the story. The questions (part 5) the storyteller asks the listener is where the real work begins. These questions should be carefully structured to initiate discussion. It is the discussion time after the story—prompted by the questions—that should be filled with meaningful dialog, discussion, and discovery. These questions connect the misconception with the story. A Scripture memory verse (part 6) is optional, depending on the situational context and the engagement level of the listener. The verse could be offered as a summary of the story or as a reinforcement to the biblical point of the story. Lastly, the hook question (part 7) is an unanswered question from the storyteller used to keep the listener thinking about the story and considering personal application of the story until the next story time. It is like the proverbial small pebble in the sandal that is annoying until it is resolved in the listener's mind. These are the words the Holy Spirit can use to keep the listener personally engaged in the topic. This overview of the seven steps is now presented in greater detail.

Identifying Misconceptions Is Central to the Task

When beginning a Bible study to prepare a story lesson, ask "Which character or people group is responding according to their wrong belief or worldview perspective?" Invest a significant amount of time identifying these misconceptions, and don't be satisfied with identifying just one. The answer is not always what seems obvious at the beginning of the story. Even the primary misconceptions may remain undetected or disguised until later reactions and responses from the characters reveal other misconceptions at play. Seek to find the misconception that appears to be motivating the story characters and your listeners. In each of the ninety stories in this book, there are at least two and usually three misconceptions identified, one or more of which may be affecting your listeners. Like the story of the good Samaritan, it was Jesus's recognition of the teacher's confusion about "neighbor" that shaped Jesus's purpose for the story. If Jesus hadn't recognized the expert's misconception, the expert teacher would have walked away from the encounter remaining convinced of his own justification.

The first objective for a storyteller is to engage the listeners so they identify with the characters and events in the story. Jesus told stories that quickly engaged his listeners because the story was relevant and compelling to them. He never told stories because he liked them, they were "interesting," or because they were packed with so many theological insights that could develop in so many directions. Rather, he told the story that was *the right choice for the listener* to engage the story quickly. It must be relevant to the listeners' lives at the time. Jesus overwhelmed his audience at the Sermon on the Mount by calling out questions they could not answer because they were thinking about physical solutions. Jesus saw they weren't including the spiritual component (Matt 5:21–44; lesson J-14). It brought them into his message, because they realized they didn't have answers for issues they previously had thought they understood.

Specifically identifying the misconceptions guides the story designer's decisions about what to include, minimize, or cut from the story to keep it focused on the issue and still make it simple, short, and easily retold. The designer must be careful not to delete any information that would help the listeners to discover the truths and the misconceptions for themselves.

Always express misconceptions for each story as a positive concept from the listener's perspective (though it is a misconception from the designer's perspective!). The misconception statements presented in this book are unavoidably influenced by this author's age, experience, education, and culture. Therefore, do not uncritically accept them as suitable for your listeners' experiences and culture. However, they are presented to serve as a model for your own lesson preparation and adaptation.

Identifying the Passage Boundaries Brings Needed Focus

A story must have a beginning and an end. There is a temptation when choosing the passage limits to add just another verse or two to potentially expand into another area of theological ideas—as if it were bonus information. But the criterion for including any verse is how well it addresses the misconception. Any additional "bonus verses" should be included as a different topic in a different story lesson.

It is important not to jeopardize the biblical story in its simplicity and directness—particularly for those listeners who would like to tell the story to their friends and relatives. The passage(s) listed for each story provides authentication for anyone's questions about the source of the story content. Again, resist the temptations to extend the story limits because you are familiar with the story and know "what comes next." But keep the story as brief and direct as possible while presenting a biblical response to the misconception(s).

Identifying the Main Parts Aids the Storyteller

An interesting story must have rapid forward movement. Breaking the story into sections, or main parts, helps the storyteller stay on track. The main parts aren't an outline of the story (outlines are favored by literate-preference learners but not oral-preference learners), but they provide an abbreviated guide for the storyteller to remain on task and keep moving the story forward to the next section or part.

It is particularly helpful for those with a literate background to have a scene associated with each section. Returning to the topic of using storyboarding, visualize a scene for each main part of the story. I once taught a story containing several geographic references. I attached those references to furniture that was in the room. I found it very helpful to walk around the

Creating an Oral Story Lesson

room to the chair or tables, describing what happened at each location. It made visualizing and repeating the conversations and scenes much easier.

These advantages of telling stories orally and visually contrasts with literate-preference teachers whose dependence upon words becomes an exercise in remembering or memorizing the exact words used in the narrative. Avoid designing more than four parts or stages to a story; more information than contained in four story sections will be difficult for new, younger generations of storytellers to retain.

Telling the Story

The storyteller must bring the listeners into the story as quickly as possible by becoming personally engaged with the story and characters—but not into the storyteller's *performance.* How can the storyteller recognize when the line between engagement and performance has been crossed? First, remember that the purpose of telling the story is to provide a model for the listeners to become storytellers themselves. If the reaction of the listeners is that they could never tell or perform a story like that storyteller, the primary purpose of reproduction is lost. But if the reaction of the listeners is that they could imitate the storyteller just as effectively, then the objective of reproducing another storyteller is attainable. In short, make the story delivery energetic enough that the listeners are engaged in the story, but not so skilled in the delivery that it discourages the listeners from attempting to imitate the model.

The stories in this collection are intended to be told to listeners who are likely oral-preference learners. Research reports as many as 80 percent of the world's population prefer to learn through nonliterate methods such as art, dance, song, drama, video, architecture, or listening. God used all those nonliterate teaching methods in the Scriptures. This book encourages storytelling because its effectiveness is not dependent on personal talent or artistry skills. However, it's undeniable that this book you are holding is appropriate for literate but not oral learners. The purpose for printing this book was to provide an initial model of how simple, short, and focused the story lessons could be for first-generation story designers and storytellers. Being oral-*preference* learners does not mean the listeners *cannot* read or write, but that they *prefer* to process information through nonliterate means. Reading and preparing the lessons in this book helps the process of transitioning to oral delivery so the next generation can reach oral-preference learners.

Why would it matter whether you are talking to literate or nonliterate listeners? It matters because oral and literate learners process information differently. They store and recall information differently because they use different practices and methods to categorize information. They communicate information differently. The literate-preference learner wants to get to the point of any story or presentation as quickly and directly as possible and is frustrated by wordiness that just slows the process to get to the point. Typically, they would be pleased with bullet-point summaries if it gets them to the point of the story more quickly.

In contrast, the nonliterate learner responds that the point of the story is the story itself. As for the danger of wordiness, oral-preference learners enjoy the variety and color of the words, allowing the words to lead to different discoveries and new thoughts for themselves. Bullet points and outlines destroy the whole point of discovering new ideas, betraying their underlying belief that all the points have been presented, concluded, and are now settled. Whereas literate learners think in straight lines and are frustrated with repeated words, phrases, or ideas, oral-preference learners think in circles and the contexts of the story and don't object to repetition because it allows thinking about the same issues from different perspectives. They enjoy the trip and don't mind the detours.

Learning preference also directly affects evangelism and missionary strategy because it plays a role in communication. The teaching preference of the teacher must match with the learning preference of the learner, or the likelihood of the effectiveness of the communication is reduced. The stories will not be as easily stored, recalled, and retold as first modeled by an earlier spiritual generation using different teaching and learning preferences. The entire learning process must be comfortable and accessible if it is to be easily repeatable and effective in creating new generations.

Creating Conversations through Questions

The misconception(s) that first defined the issue for the story lesson now makes a return to form the questions that will generate discussions about the story and the characters' beliefs exposed in the story and raise the beliefs of the listeners to a conscious level. This is not the time for the storyteller to state the misconception driving the story or to summarize the story according to the storyteller's own personal beliefs. Rather, this is a discussion time for the listeners to interpret what they believed about different reactions based upon perspectives that, perhaps, they hadn't even considered five minutes earlier. Observing at least a biblical and a non-biblical response to interpret the story requires a thoughtful discussion and different interpretations. This discussion time is not to confront one another but to indirectly encourage listeners to consider new conclusions and recognize inconsistencies in their own beliefs.

Because no one can change another's worldview, the most a storyteller or teacher can do is influence listeners to reconsider the ability or the inability of their own worldviews to answer the challenges exposed in the story. This is the most critical part of the entire story lesson, and it is done by encouraging dialogue concerning the characters in the story. In a question and answer format, the listener is not feeling personally challenged or attacked because the arguments are indirect; they are voiced by the characters and not directly between the storyteller and the listener. That's why the best strategy to initiate the discussion is through questions.

Each story lesson suggests questions, but select the best three or four questions for your situation, or develop your own questions. Having begun with identifying the primary misconceptions for the story, these misconceptions now are very useful to shape the lesson's questions. Take each misconception and ask which question would sharpen the listeners' curiosity about it. Which questions will cause the listeners to describe the issue as it appears in the story? Which questions will expose the inadequacy or the inconsistency of how they would have previously defined the issue? Would the central point that made the issue a misconception be recognized by asking the question?

Questions can be either story specific or general. The questions offered in this book are story specific. The problem with being story specific is that the questions must be remembered by the storyteller as the story itself. That places an additional burden on the new believer a spiritual generation later. The value of being story specific is that the storyteller can help lead the discussion and the focus of the story. By contrast, examples of general questions are: "What did you like about the story? What did you learn about God? What did you learn about man? What bothered you about the situation? Do you recall a similar situation faced by the characters?" Once these questions are memorized, they can be applied to any story without additional memory demands.

The Value of Scripture Memory

Suggesting a verse for the listener to memorize provides an opening for the Holy Spirit to use the living word of God to bring about change. But the storyteller must be aware if asking the person to memorize Scripture is appropriate. Depending on the situation and the responsiveness of the listener, it may be best to offer it as an option.

The Hook Question Is the Stone in the Sandal

The hook question is given by the storyteller but left unanswered with the listener. It is an application question that personalizes the story to the listener. Leaving the question unanswered allows the listener to explore different responses while engaged in different actual activities. A good "hook" will keep the listener thinking about the story and how the story personally affects the listener until it's time for another story lesson. Each question is given in the first person (I) and not the second person (you), as if the listeners are asking themselves the question for personal reflection. It is much easier to create these questions in the second person, but you will discover that the tone of the first-person question is uncomfortably direct to the listener and that—though more difficult—the discipline of using the first person will result in better questions.

The Story Selection Process

The Catalog of Misconceptions

The following table lists 160 misconceptions identified in this collection of ninety stories. Notice that all the misconceptions are stated positively as the potential listeners may state the concept. But there is an error within each statement. More or differently voiced misconceptions may arise for each different culture, so do not interpret this list of misconceptions as complete or definitive.

Prayerfully read through each of the misconceptions. Among the people you know, question yourself if that is something you believe one of your friends would say. Write this friend's name next to that misconception in the middle column. In the far right column is the story lesson that would lead to discussing that misconception (remember the OT prefix is for the Old Testament source; the J prefix is for the life of Jesus; and the NT prefix is for the New Testament sources).

Creating an Oral Story Lesson

You have now identified the potential listener, identified and targeted the misconception, and chosen the related story lesson. Now it is time for focused prayer for the lesson encounter with the listener. It's also the time to practice telling the story and learning the questions until you're comfortable with them. Edit the story as necessary so you're comfortable with every word. Also make the story comfortable for the listener to repeat the story to their own friends. The best preparatory help you could have would be to form a small group of at least four others who will join you in practicing telling the story with each other.

Misconception	*Listener's Name*	*Lesson*
Creation through a Creator is an unproven myth.		OT 1
Creation was the result of chance, time, and evolution.		OT 1
Creation was without purpose or design.		OT 1
Man's relationship to God is based upon man's performance of religious duties.		OT 2
Mankind, as a part of creation, always seeks to overcome creation.		OT 2
Man did not dishonor God though he disobeyed God.		OT 2
Comparing God's blessings on others reveals God's level of favor or disfavor with me.		OT 3
Fulfilling sacrificial duties guarantees God's pleasure and acceptance.		OT 3
Self-justification of personal righteousness indicates God's level of expected satisfaction.		OT 3
God's goal for creation ended with Adam and Eve's disobedience in the garden.		OT 4
Noah was spared from judgment because of his own goodness and righteousness.		OT 4
God wanted to punish sinful man and vent his anger.		OT 4
God made a covenant with Abram because of Abram's personal righteousness.		OT 5
Abram's righteous life after receiving God's promise earned the land he would receive.		OT 5
Man plans strategies and timetables to fulfill God's promises and purposes for him.		OT 6
Ishmael was the promised son through Hagar.		OT 6
Man's actions can block, postpone, or delay God's ideal fulfillment of his promises.		OT 6

Ninety Biblical Story Lessons for Adults

Misconception	Listener's Name	Lesson
A covenant isn't confirmed until it is fulfilled.		OT 7
God's promised commitment to a person ends when that person dies.		OT 7
God uses only people of integrity and compassion to accomplish his plans.		OT 8
God adjusts his plans according to the decisions or responses of people.		OT 8
Being a victim of deceit or not experiencing blessings is always a sign of God's displeasure.		OT 8
Negative or positive events in our lives are due to fate.		OT 9
Deceitful or evil actions against us must be defeated or overcome by our own actions.		OT 9
Evil intentions against us always end in evil results.		OT 9
Ease of labor is more important than freedom of worship.		OT 10
Divine promises become irrelevant and forgotten over generations.		OT 10
Seeing or experiencing a miracle will convince one to believe in God's promises.		OT 10
God is concerned only about people's spiritual lives, leaving people to satisfy their own physical needs.		OT 11
God's frustrations with man's constant grumbling produce only discipline and judgment.		OT 11
God's laws are burdensome and demanding, because God is a stern King.		OT 11
All those who lead have equal authority.		OT 12
Leaders evaluate other leaders according to their own personal standards or motivations.		OT 12
Leaders assume their leadership position because of their self-appointment.		OT 12
Man remains faithful to his promises.		OT 13
God forgives all sin without anger or consequences.		OT 13
Offering sacrifices to God earns his favor.		OT 14
God requires sacrifices as a dutiful requirement.		OT 14
Sacrifices to God influence God's willingness to bless his people.		OT 14
Sacrifices are all the same and serve the same purpose.		OT 14
The power of nations or kingdoms, not God, determines the nations' or kingdoms' own homelands.		OT 15

CREATING AN ORAL STORY LESSON

Misconception	Listener's Name	Lesson
An entire nation does not bear the consequences of a few, nonelected leaders.		OT 15
God judges and disciplines only national leaders but not an entire nation.		OT 15
God uses only his chosen righteous ones to accomplish his plans.		OT 16
God uses only his written words (Scripture) to reveal himself.		OT 16
Personal sins affect only the person who sinned; others do not bear the consequences.		OT 17
The causes of calamity and fear of even worse events can be resolved only by man.		OT 17
Our own knowledge provides sufficient understanding to make wise decisions.		OT 18
Our small and often irrelevant personal acts and attitudes are unnoticed by God.		OT 18
God's attention is focused only on the large, consequential acts that fulfill his plans.		OT 18
God is intolerant of our lack of faith.		OT 19
God calls only faith-filled people to lead in times of crisis.		OT 19
Influential fathers should appoint their children to continue their legacy, even if unqualified or unfit.		OT 20
Children of respected ruling leaders will faithfully continue their parents' honorable leadership.		OT 20
God's call to offer sacrifices is our greatest measure of devotion.		OT 21
God doesn't keep track of offenses against his people forever.		OT 21
God's leadership appointments always have his blessings and are unchanging.		OT 22
Confidence in God's calling still requires personal strategy to achieve the call.		OT 22
Every strategic benefit that comes to you should be pursued without regard to other influences.		OT 22
Confidence from past victories ensures future successes.		OT 23
Private sins can be hidden from God and the public.		OT 23
Forgiveness of sins protects from future consequences of those sins.		OT 23

Ninety Biblical Story Lessons for Adults

Misconception	Listener's Name	Lesson
The extent of sin's effects can be safely tested, controlled, and limited by man's choices.		OT 24
Wisdom is more valuable and powerful than obedience.		OT 24
Practicing religious duties always results in spiritual power, blessings, and victory for the worshipper.		OT 25
Offering religious rituals will satisfy the people that the god will provide peace and safety.		OT 25
Political leadership is based upon power and not compassion.		OT 25
Familiar spiritual rituals are unquestioned and repeated even if ineffective.		OT 26
Courageous spiritual leaders have no spiritual weaknesses.		OT 26
Measure God's work by your own firsthand experience.		OT 26
Victory is assured for the strongest and the smartest army.		OT 27
The spiritual realm does not affect the physical realm of politics and warfare.		OT 27
Politics and military power determine world events.		OT 28
Religious practices and faithfulness do not influence world events.		OT 28
God does not consider personal or national obedience when determining peace or war.		OT 28
God can influence the present but not determine the future.		OT 28
God leaves those who have been disciplined to recover without his help.		OT 29
God permits nations and empires to control their own plans and sovereignty apart from him.		OT 29
God no longer cares about the land, because his Spirit left the temple and he removed the people.		OT 29
God's story was completed when the people returned to their homeland from their exile.		OT 30
God no longer cares about Jerusalem and the land; he has left them both to rule themselves like other nations.		OT 30
Jesus's birth announcement was unknown at the time but created only after Jesus became famous.		J 1
God cannot appear in flesh but only in spirit.		J 1

Creating an Oral Story Lesson

Misconception	Listener's Name	Lesson
Jesus was a prophet and was not identified as a Savior, Son of God, or Eternal King until after his death.		J 1
Jesus revealed his powers only to those who believed in him.		J 2
Jesus was powerless to overrule natural laws.		J 2
Past experiences determine future ministry.		J 3
Obedience to Jesus's commands requires first having faith.		J 3
Being a sinner disqualifies a person from being called to ministry.		J 3
Jesus was not actively involved in common activities or needs.		J 4
We are limited by the supplies and preparations we bring to a needed activity.		J 4
Miracles are always very public to gain notice.		J 4
Jesus cannot change physical matter or laws.		J 5
Jesus is unaware of everyone's situation and the needs of those who are beyond his presence.		J 5
Jesus cannot give full attention to everyone's needs or situations at once.		J.5
What happens to Jesus's followers is beyond Jesus's control.		J 6
Natural dangers are outside Jesus's powers to control.		J 6
Though Jesus has compassion for those struggling, he does not protect them from those struggles.		J 6
Jesus's healings were psychologically influenced.		J 7
Jesus's healings were adjustments made naturally by physical manipulations.		J 7
Jesus's healings were spiritual battles with demons.		J 7
Jesus's healings were performed as magic.		J 7
Healing is granted to those who are worthy.		J 7
Believing is based upon personally seeing a miracle.		J 7
Disabilities are God's judgments for the sins of either the disabled or their parents.		J 8
Peoples' physical condition reflects their spiritual condition.		J 8
Miracles cannot prove divine authority unless they also fit in man's theological categories.		J 8

Ninety Biblical Story Lessons for Adults

Misconception	Listener's Name	Lesson
Those who report a personal witness of Jesus are not persecuted.		J 8
God is unaffected by our personal tragedies or crises.		J 9
Everyone is responsible to satisfy their own personal needs.		J 9
Death is more powerful than Jesus's ability to heal.		J 10
Jesus's influence and power were limited to teaching and healing.		J 10
Jesus was only a prophet who could heal those who were ill.		J 11
Resurrection is a one-time event for all people at the end of the age.		J 11
Jesus's response was influenced by his emotions.		J 11
Treat your enemies with the same hostility they treat you or others.		J 12
You must love, greet, or do good things only to those who love you.		J 12
Hate your enemies.		J 12
Do not lend money to those who will not repay you.		J 12
Maintaining personal ritual cleanliness is more important than serving others.		J 13
Neighbors share equal social status with another.		J 13
Neighbors share a common cultural identity.		J 13
Common cultural understanding of religious sayings should be unquestioned.		J 14
It is possible to obey all Jewish law perfectly as taught by religious teachers.		J 14
Our righteous standing before God is determined by the performance of religious duties and perfect obedience of commands.		J 14
I am righteous because I don't commit evil deeds like other people.		J 15
I am righteous, because I practice religious duties like prayer, fasting, and tithing.		J 15
I work to gain more righteousness than other people.		J 15
It is justifiable and good financial management to preserve my wealth rather than to give it away.		J 16
It is more important to increase my possessions for the future than to give to God in the present.		J 16

Creating an Oral Story Lesson

Misconception	Listener's Name	Lesson
Increasing wealth for my future is good financial planning and never greedy.		J 16
Religious cultural traditions establish unquestioned foundational truths.		J 17
True worship of God is formed out of cultural practices rather than religious questions.		J 17
God does not seek after us, but we must seek after God.		J 17
Honor and rewards must be earned by faithfulness.		J 18
Restoration can be earned back by the dishonored.		J 18
A motivation for obedience is earning a reward.		J 18
We are able to protect ourselves; we have no need of someone to protect us.		J 19
We are unable to hear Jesus's words and teachings.		J 19
We have no enemies who are trying to scatter us from others like us.		J 19
Leaders have all the power and authority to appoint other leaders.		J 20
Great leaders should be powerful, to enforce their authority and will upon their subjects.		J 20
Jesus will establish a political rule in his future kingdom.		J 20
Miracles do not prove God's involvement.		J 21
Miracles are not evidence of God's approval.		J 21
Miracles are dependent on personal faith and not on intercessors who have faith.		J 21
The highest priority in demonstrating righteousness is obedience to the law's requirements.		J 22
Any activity of love, service, or compassion is defined as work that violates Sabbath rest.		J 22
Holiness and righteousness are revealed by refusing any activity on the Sabbath.		J 22
Compassion or goodness is secondary to lawful obedience.		J 22
Repeating traditional religious practices approved by religious leadership assures righteousness before God.		J 23
Traditional religious practices always follow scriptural commands.		J 23
A person's righteousness is always revealed by the company the person keeps.		J 24

Ninety Biblical Story Lessons for Adults

Misconception	Listener's Name	Lesson
Calling to spiritual repentance is only for those who are spiritually righteous.		J 24
Keeping a pure spiritual reputation is better than being a friend to those lacking a good reputation.		J 24
Increasing personal power and influence is more important than speaking truth or doing good.		J 25
Washing hands makes a person clean before God.		J 25
Jesus was unable to overcome the authority and power of both political and religious leadership.		J 26
Jesus lost control of the situation.		J 26
Jesus did not die on the cross but caused an illusion for another to die in his place.		J 27
Jesus was executed quickly.		J 27
Jesus was executed privately under Roman control.		J 27
Life in Jerusalem continued normally when Jesus died on the cross.		J 28
Events that happened when Jesus died were seen by only a few and can all be explained away.		J 28
Jesus's dead body was hidden by the disciples who then reported that Jesus had risen.		J 28
Jesus's body was stolen and hidden by Jesus's followers, who then created the myth of the resurrection.		J 29
The nature of Jesus's resurrected body was the same one as the body that had just been killed on the cross.		J 29
Only Jesus's disciples testified they saw the resurrected Jesus.		J 30
Jesus appeared only immediately after his resurrection.		J 30
Jesus's resurrection was only his spirit and not his physical body.		J 30
Speaking in an unknown foreign language is not a miraculous sign, because it can be explained naturally.		NT 1
The disciples could not prove or give an explanation to confirm these new events.		NT 1
Financial support is the primary need of the physically disabled.		NT 2
Power and intimidation can overcome contrary facts.		NT 2
Personal spiritual power and godliness enable healing of the sick.		NT 2

Creating an Oral Story Lesson

Misconception	Listener's Name	Lesson
Gaining honor and respect is a priority, even if misrepresentation or deception is used.		NT 3
God can be deceived.		NT 3
God does not know or challenge my personal wealth or the amount I choose to give to others.		NT 3
God judges people according to the amount they chose to give.		NT 3
Authorities can affect God's plans, using persecution through mobs, intimidation, jail, and even death.		NT 4
Persecution and fear reduce the number of believers and commitment level of those believers oppressed.		NT 4
Persecutors are so committed they will never change their minds.		NT 5
God calls to lead others only those who have proven their loyalty to him and service to others.		NT 5
Those God chooses to lead others are protected from suffering and greatly blessed.		NT 5
Observing the past actions of people justifies anticipating their future response.		NT 6
People don't change lifetime commitments to their beliefs.		NT 6
Expectations of future events are dependent upon past events.		NT 6
Successful ministry is defined by counting the number of new believers.		NT 7
Unsuccessful ministry outreach is a result of only one new believer.		NT 7
A single person from a different race from a foreign country is not a fruitful ministry objective.		NT 7
The benefits of Jesus's messiahship are only for Jews but irrelevant to gentiles.		NT 8
Personal righteousness is based upon avoiding all unclean actions.		NT 8
God doesn't need man to tell his revelation; he can fully reveal himself by himself.		NT 8
The government determines who will be persecuted, prosecuted, punished, and killed.		NT 9
The government is more powerful than believers' prayers.		NT 9
Miracles always lead to belief.		NT 10

Ninety Biblical Story Lessons for Adults

Misconception	Listener's Name	Lesson
Believers can independently teach and organize ministry without accountability to the church.		NT 10
When God sets you aside from one ministry, start your own ministry.		NT 10
Miracles always accurately interpret God's revelation and confirm his authority.		NT 11
Crowds slowly reach reasoned conclusions and remain consistent in their blessings or condemnations.		NT 11
Listeners always decide about Christianity slowly and deliberately.		NT 11
God's acceptance for salvation is based upon fully obeying Moses's law.		NT 12
Non-Jews must observe the Jewish laws and traditions like Jews to be righteous before God.		NT 12
The prophets' words in Scripture emphasized that salvation belonged to the Jews and not to the gentiles.		NT 12
Being persecuted, tortured, or jailed weakens a person's commitment to worship and serve God.		NT 13
Doing good for others always results in appreciation.		NT 13
Creating temples, idols, and precious objects of worship pleases God and gains his favor.		NT 14
There is a god beyond man's knowledge who should be honored as the unknown god.		NT 14
God requires and expects people to craft idols and other tokens of worship for him.		NT 14
A leader of the church is expected to increase his power, honor, and influence.		NT 15
Young believers must place their loyalty and trust in their leaders and teachers.		NT 15
Followers should promote their leaders and teachers as superior to all other leaders.		NT 15
God judges by favoring one people over others.		NT 16
God's authority as judge allows him to favor people groups he prefers to love.		NT 16
Righteousness results from rigorously obeying the laws of righteousness.		NT 16
There is no resurrection from the dead.		NT 17
The body we have on earth is the body that will enter heaven.		NT 17

CREATING AN ORAL STORY LESSON

Misconception	Listener's Name	Lesson
Only a few people saw the ghost of Jesus and not his resurrected body.		NT 17
The Christian gospel is exclusive to Jews only.		NT 18
Righteousness and identification of the Messiah come through obedience to Jewish laws and commands.		NT 18
Greeks will always be foreigners to Jews and Jesus because they worshipped idols and foreign gods in their past.		NT 18
Words alone have spiritual authority to create and control results for either blessings or curses.		NT 19
Authoritative power is assumed when speaking the name of God or Jesus.		NT 19
We receive salvation by faith but are perfected in righteousness through our efforts.		NT 20
The Holy Spirit makes us righteous based upon our obedience to Jewish law.		NT 20
Abraham is a blessing only for his own descendants.		NT 20
Persecutions will stop the progress of the church.		NT 21
Preaching Jesus will bring only respect and honor.		NT 21
Persecution brings discouragement.		NT 21
Personal clothing choices always accurately reflect people's character.		NT 22
The ability to communicate religious convictions indicates a person's religious commitment.		NT 22
Personal evaluations and judgments about others don't have a moral context.		NT 22
Honor and dignity should be given only to those who have earned it.		NT 22
God protects those who believe in Jesus from experiencing shame and mistreatment.		NT 23
Retaliation is the best way to protect honor when falsely accused, shamed, or abused.		NT 23
The shame of dishonor has no positive benefit.		NT 23
The resurrection of Jesus reveals the successful completion of Jesus's mission.		NT 24
The resurrection of Jesus was a disproved hoax.		NT 24
The resurrection of Jesus emphasizes Jesus but not his followers.		NT 24

Ninety Biblical Story Lessons for Adults

Misconception	Listener's Name	Lesson
Trust the wisdom of those who are powerful and influential to guide your life decisions.		NT 25
Trust Jewish history and spiritual signs to guide your decisions.		NT 25
Those who are weak and despised have no value or influence on others.		NT 25
Wealth and power indicate God's blessing.		NT 25
Those with public gifts should likewise be publicly honored.		NT 26
Those who only want to quietly serve others make their own decisions when to serve.		NT 26
Believers can identify their own gifts according to their own desires.		NT 26
Believers choose when to use, how to use, and when to limit the use of their gifts.		NT 26
Anyone can resist temptation and sin empowered by their own will.		NT 27
There is no evidence that people are too spiritually weak to resist sin.		NT 27
Those who rely on their own power are able to defeat spiritual temptations or attacks.		NT 27
A hope and a wish are the same thing.		NT 28
No one can fulfill a promise, because future events are unknown and uncontrolled.		NT 28
Nothing can protect everyone from persecution.		NT 28
Keeping in fellowship with God requires staying perfectly sinless.		NT 29
Confessing sins means making a list to name them all.		NT 29
Being guilty of sin removes the ability to be restored to walk in God's light again.		NT 29
Symbolic language is used to describe "real-world" items in detail.		NT 30
Evil purposes are not repetitive or universal across time and location.		NT 30
Understanding the historic, constant presence of good and evil in the world enables believers to know how to accept and relate to evil.		NT 30

Chapter 2

Thirty Old Testament Story Lessons

OT 1: God Created a Pure and Perfect Universe

The Misconceptions

- Creation through a Creator is an unproven myth.
- Creation was the result of chance, time, and evolution.
- Creation was without purpose or design.

The Passage: Gen 1:1—2:25

The Main Points

1. God created everything by his word and declared everything good.
2. God first created a separate place and home for each living thing he created.
3. Lastly, God created Adam and Eve, who were naked and unashamed.
4. God named Adam, and then Adam named the woman and all the creatures.

The Story

The earth was in darkness and unformed and completely covered by water. Then God spoke, and by his word he separated light from darkness, land from water, and daylight from night's darkness. He made creatures to live in the seas and the air, and animals and cattle herds to live in the land. All the vegetation, creatures, and livestock were to reproduce themselves. And God said everything was good.

Then God said, "Let us make man in our image and likeness and let them rule over all the animals that had been made." God named the man Adam, and then Adam named the woman Eve. And God gave authority to Adam to name all the other animals God had created. He put Adam and Eve in a beautiful garden he had already made for them. The garden included two trees in the middle of it—one called the tree of knowledge of good and evil, and the second called the tree of life. Adam and Eve were allowed to eat the fruit from any of the trees except the tree of knowledge of good and evil. Adam and Eve were naked but unashamed, and God often visited them in this garden.

The Questions

- What did God require of Adam and Eve to enjoy his presence in the garden? (Not what they were required *not* to do, but what were they to do?)
- Why didn't Adam's duties include offering sacrifices or other religious practices?
- Which clues reveal God's intention in creating Adam and Eve? Do you think God still has that intention, or did Adam and Eve's later actions force God to change his intention?
- Why do you think God created man on a different day than all the other animals?

The Scripture Memory: Ps 8:5–6

The Hook Questions

Which thoughts about heaven do I have that would be satisfied by living in the garden as Adam and Eve did?

Do I have any other thoughts about what I wish were present in heaven, other than what God provided in the garden?

OT 2: Questioning God's Goodness Brought Sin

The Misconceptions

- Man's relationship to God is based upon man's performance of religious duties.
- Mankind, as a part of creation, always seeks to overcome creation.
- Man did not dishonor God though he disobeyed God.

The Passage: Gen 3:1–24

The Main Points

1. When alone, Eve was tempted by Satan, who twisted God's command not to eat from the tree of knowledge of good and evil. But she ate the fruit and then tempted Adam to dishonor God by also disobeying the command.
2. Because of their rebellion, Adam and Eve felt guilt, shame, and fear when they heard God calling out to them.
3. God ordered Adam and Eve out of the garden, cursed the serpent, and gave the woman the pain of childbirth and the man the toil of working hard soil. Before leaving, God killed an animal and clothed Adam and Eve with its skin.

The Story

Satan, an enemy of God, appeared as a deceptive snake and asked Eve about God's command not to eat fruit from the tree of knowledge of good and evil, twisting God's command until Eve doubted God and believed eating from the tree would allow her to know good and evil just like God did. She disbelieved God's warning that she would die if she ate the fruit. She saw how good the fruit looked, so she ate it and then encouraged Adam to eat it also.

After eating the fruit, Adam and Eve heard God calling to them in the garden and, for the first time, realized they were naked, ashamed, and now fearful of God. So they hid from God. When God asked where they were, they explained they were naked and had hidden, which revealed their disobedience. Adam blamed Eve for tempting his disobedience, and Eve blamed the serpent.

God cursed the serpent so it would crawl on the ground and gave Eve the pain of childbirth, while Adam's gardening became hard work of hard soil. After killing an animal to give the skin for clothing, God ordered Adam and Eve out of the garden and then posted an angel to keep man from returning to the garden and possibly eating from the tree of life.

The Questions

- How did Adam and Eve's innocence turn to guilt? How could they restore their own innocence?
- How could Adam and Eve restore their own honor?
- How could Adam and Eve restore their relationship with God from the fear they now experienced?
- Which elements of the story were most significant to you? Why?

The Scripture Memory: Gen 3:10; Ps 8:5–6

The Hook Questions

Do I have both the desire and the ability to eliminate any feelings of guilt, shame, or fear I have?

Do I desire to see God being worshipped and honored among all people, including my family and friends?

OT 3: Cain's Jealousy Resulted in Abel's Murder

The Misconceptions

- Comparing God's blessings on others reveals God's level of favor or disfavor with me.
- Fulfilling sacrificial duties guarantees God's pleasure and acceptance.
- Self-justification of personal righteousness indicates God's level of expected satisfaction.

The Passage: Gen 4:2–16

The Main Points

1. Cain worked the fields, and Abel cared for the flocks.
2. Both Cain and Abel offered God sacrifices from the harvests of their work. God accepted Abel's sacrifice but not Cain's, resulting in Cain's anger.
3. God warned Cain to control his anger, but he didn't and killed Abel in the field.
4. God punished Cain for Abel's murder and sent Cain from God's presence.

The Story

Adam and Eve had a son named Cain, followed by a second son named Abel. Cain raised crops, and Abel took care of the flocks. After some time, Cain gathered some of the harvest from the ground, which he offered to God. Abel brought the choicest fat of the firstborn of his flock to offer God. God accepted Abel's offering but not Cain's offering, which made Cain angry.

God questioned Cain why he was angry, which was obvious from Cain's face. God told Cain, "If you do well, your face will be lifted up. But if you don't do well, then sin is crouching over you to master you. But you must master it."

But Cain rejected God's advice, and he grew angrier and angrier until he killed his brother out in the field. When God asked Cain where Abel was, Cain lied and said, "I do not know where he is. Am I his keeper?"

God then said, "What have you done? Your brother's blood calls out to me from the ground. Now you are cursed from the ground. Your work breaking the ground will be unfruitful for you. You will no longer have a home and instead will only wander upon the earth!"

Cain cried out, "This punishment is too great! Whoever finds me will kill me!" But God said, "Whoever kills you, I will take vengeance sevenfold on him. And I will put a sign on you that will warn everyone not to kill you." And so Cain departed from God's presence.

The Questions

1. Was Cain angry with God or with Abel? How did his anger begin and result in Abel's murder?
2. How did Cain and Abel's preparations for offering a sacrifice indicate their attitudes toward it?
3. Do you think this is a story about attitudes toward offerings or about comparing yourself to others, which can lead to jealousy, anger, or murder?
4. What does God reveal about his approach to correcting people who are not pleasing him?

The Scripture Memory: 1 Sam 15:22

The Hook Question

Which sacrifices do I believe I offered to God but for which I don't have assurance they were acceptable to God?

OT 4: God Flooded Earth but Rescued Noah

The Misconceptions

- God's goal for creation ended with Adam and Eve's disobedience in the garden.
- Noah was spared from judgment because of his own goodness and righteousness.
- God wanted to punish sinful man and vent his anger.

The Passages: Gen 6:5–22; 7:1—9:20

The Main Parts

1. God cursed the land because of man's evil acts.
2. God's sorrow and pain from evil and the curse of land motivated him to judge all the earth.
3. God chose Noah, his family, and animals to escape judgment in the ark.
4. God made a covenant never to curse the land or destroy all life with a flood again.

The Story

God cursed the ground after Adam and Eve disobeyed God and then cursed it again after Cain murdered his brother, Abel. The cursed ground made work painful and hard. Adam and Eve had a third son, Seth, whose descendant was Lamech, the father of Noah. At Noah's birth, Lamech said, "This one will give us rest and comfort from the sorrowful and painful work of our hands."

Though the cursed land caused sorrow and pain to man, man's evil caused great sorrow and pain to God. Instead of providing rest and comfort for man's pain, God chose to judge man for the evil by making a flood that would wipe man off the earth. But God graciously let one man and his family escape the judgment—a man who was righteous, blameless, and walked with God. So God directed Noah to build a large boat, called an ark, to protect Noah, his family, and male and female animals of each kind to repopulate the land after the flood.

When Noah had completed the ark, God made male and female animals enter the ark and then directed Noah and his family to enter it with their families. Then God closed the door and the rain began, raining forty days and nights. The flood was so complete, it took seven months before the water allowed the ark to rest on a mountaintop, and then many more months before it was dry enough to leave the ark. Noah tested the ground by sending out ravens and doves. One time a dove brought back an olive leaf that proved life had begun again. The next week, the dove didn't return at all. Then God directed them to leave the ark.

Noah's first act was to offer a sacrifice to God, and its smell pleased God. God told Noah's family they should be fruitful and multiply throughout the earth. God made a covenant promise that he would never again curse the ground or destroy all life by a flood, and the sign of the covenant would be the rainbow in the sky. All the families and nations of the world descended from Noah's three sons.

The Questions

1. Compare how working the land before the flood changed from Adam's work in the garden. Why?
2. What did you discover about God's emotions?
3. What did Noah do to escape God's judgment of the world in this time before God revealed his laws to man?
4. What motivated God to protect Noah, his family, and the animals?

The Scripture Memory: Gen 8:21

The Hook Question

If God has a plan for mankind, can anything stop him from accomplishing it?

OT 5: Abram Called by God to Make a Nation

The Misconceptions

- God made a covenant with Abram because of Abram's personal righteousness.
- Abram's righteous life after receiving God's promise earned the land he would receive.

The Passage: Gen 11:27—14:20

The Main Parts

1. Abram's life before the call
2. God's call to Abram to leave
3. Abram's arrival in Canaan and then Egypt
4. Abram's separation from Lot, who was later captured and then rescued by Abram

The Story

Terah, a grandson of Noah, had three sons. He left the land of Ur of the Chaldeans where he worshipped other gods. He left for the more fertile land of Canaan. He traveled with his son, Abram; Abram's wife, Sarai; and a grandson, Lot, whose father had died. They got only as far as the city of Haran, where Terah died.

After Terah's death, God told Abram to go south to Canaan, where God would make his descendants into a great nation. God also promised that Abram would bless all the nations of the world, and God would bless those who blessed him and curse those who cursed him.

Abram believed God's promises and left for Canaan with Sarai and Lot. God counted Abram's belief as righteousness, so when they arrived in Canaan, God appeared to Abram and again promised, "I will give this land to your descendants." Abram built an altar where God appeared and a second altar in Bethel. But there was famine in the land, so Abram decided to leave Canaan and go to Egypt instead.

When they arrived in Egypt, Abram feared someone would kill him to marry Sarai, his beautiful wife, so he told her to say she was his sister instead of his wife. Egypt's Pharaoh wanted Sarai, and took her into his house, and gave Abram riches, cattle, and servants. But God struck Pharaoh and his house with diseases that caused Pharaoh to realize Abram had lied about his relationship to Sarai. Pharaoh sent her back to Abram and angrily commanded his soldiers to remove Abram, Sarah, and all they owned out of Egypt. So Abram returned to his altar in Bethel and again called upon God.

After a while, Abram became rich in silver, gold, and livestock, and Lot's herds were also growing, so the land became too small for both of them. Abram told Lot to move away but gave him his choice where to move. Lot chose the Jordan Valley, leaving Canaan for Abram. Then God commanded Abram to look in every direction in Canaan and again promised he would give the land to Abram and his descendants forever, and they would be as many as the dust on the earth. So Abram moved to the city of Hebron and built a third altar.

A few years later, four kings attacked the Jordan Valley and kidnapped Lot and his family and stole all their food and riches. Abram rescued Lot and the treasures but wouldn't accept any rewards from the kings of Sodom and Gomorrah, so only God, and not Abram, would get the glory for Abram's wealth.

The Questions

- Was Abram required to do anything to receive God's promise of receiving a homeland, an heir, and many descendants?
- Was Abram expected to fulfill the promises himself?
- What did Abram do that could have jeopardized the fulfillment of the promises?

The Scripture Memory: Gen 15:6

The Hook Question

How may Abram's response to God's promises suggest what God expects of you in response to a promised offer of eternal life?

OT 6: Abram Tested God's Promises to Him

The Misconceptions
- Man plans strategies and timetables to fulfill God's promises and purposes for him.
- Ishmael was the promised son through Hagar.
- Man's actions can block, postpone, or delay God's ideal fulfillment of his promises.

The Passages: Gen 15:1—16:15; 21:1–6; 22:1–19

The Main Parts
1. God's covenant promise of an heir, land, and descendants to Abram
2. Sarai's suggestion of an heir through Hagar
3. Sarai's miraculous birth of Isaac
4. Attempted sacrifice of the heir, Isaac

The Story

Many years after God had promised Abram descendants and land, Abram asked God, "You have given me no children, leaving only my servant to become my heir." God answered, "The servant will not be your heir. Instead, a son from your own body will be your heir, and your descendants will be as many as the stars." Abram believed God's promise, and God counted Abram's faith as righteousness.

But Abram still wondered when and how his heir would come. God answered by making a covenant promise. God directed Abram to take animals, cut them in half as an offering, and leave a path between them. Culturally, two people making a covenant promise would walk between the animal carcasses as a picture of their own punishment if either failed to fulfill their promise. God caused Abram to sleep as God walked the path between the sacrificed animals alone while declaring his promises to Abram.

But when ten years had passed without an heir, Sarai suggested Abram sleep with their young Egyptian maid, Hagar. This resulted in the birth of a son they named Ishmael. But Sarai and Hagar fought with each other until Hagar ran away. An angel of the Lord found Hagar and commanded her to return to Sarai, promising her son would become a great nation. God was with Ishmael as he grew until Hagar found him an Egyptian wife.

God again promised Abram and Sarai their heir would come through them and renamed them Abraham, meaning "father of nations," and Sarah, meaning "princess." The next year, Sarah had a son through Abraham, and they named him Isaac. On the day Isaac was weaned, Sarah and Hagar had another argument, and Abraham sent Hagar and Ishmael away from the family with a few provisions. God cared for them in the desert where Ishmael grew to manhood and Hagar found him an Egyptian wife.

Several more years had passed when God commanded Abraham to take Isaac and offer him as a sacrificial offering to God. Abraham and Isaac prepared the altar, and Isaac asked where the sacrificial lamb was. Abraham answered, "The Lord will provide." But then Abraham bound Isaac and put him on the altar and took his knife to kill him. Then God called from heaven and commanded, "Do not lay a hand on the boy. Now I know you fear God and have not withheld your son from me." Abraham then saw a ram caught in a thicket to sacrifice as a substitute for his son. God again confirmed three covenant promises to Abraham: 1) his descendants would be as many as the stars, 2) Abraham would possess the land, and 3) Abraham would bless the nations of the earth.

The Questions

- Though Abraham believed God would be faithful to fulfill his promises, how did God answer his questions about when and what he must do to see the promises fulfilled?
- How would God's different responses to Abraham's questions encourage your own faith?
- Were God's plans threatened because Sarah gave Hagar to Abraham, to have his son instead of her? How did God respond?

The Scripture Memory: Gen 22:8

The Hook Questions

If God made a promise to me, would I be comfortable waiting for its fulfillment, or would I try to fulfill God's promise on my own?

How would I know whether to keep waiting or fulfill it on my own?

OT 7: Sarah Died and Isaac Prepared to Lead

The Misconceptions
- A covenant isn't confirmed until it is fulfilled.
- God's promised commitment to a person ends when that person dies.

The Passage: Gen 23:1—25:10

The Main Parts
- The death and burial of Sarah
- Abraham's commission of his servant to get a wife for Isaac
- The servant found Rebecca, who returned with him to meet and marry Isaac.
- Abraham prepared for his own death by sending all his other children away from Isaac.

The Story

After Sarah died in Canaan, Abraham insisted on paying the local tribesmen for a tomb and received a deed for the plot despite knowing God had promised all of Canaan to him. But Abraham did not want a Canaanite wife for his son, Isaac, who was now forty years old. Instead, Abraham wanted a wife from his own family and clan, so he sent his servant back to his homeland in Ur of the Chaldeans with ten camels and expensive gifts for her family.

The servant approached the well outside Ur at evening, when women usually drew water. He prayed for God's guidance and prayed a woman would respond kindly to his request for water and also offer water for his camels. Before he finished praying, a woman came with a jar to fill with water. He asked her for water, which she gave, and then she also offered water for his camels. The servant asked the woman if her father could provide housing for the night. She introduced herself as Rebecca, the granddaughter of Abraham's brother.

The servant explained to Rebecca's brother, Laban, that he was seeking a wife for Isaac, the son of Abraham and Sarah. He explained how God had answered his prayer to identify God's choice of Rebecca for Isaac. Her family agreed that this was from the Lord, and they agreed for her to go to Isaac. The servant gave the expensive gifts to Rebecca, her mother, and Laban. Rebecca agreed to leave with the servant, with her maids.

Isaac was meditating in the field in the evening when he saw the servant returning and went to meet them. Rebecca asked who the man was approaching them, and the servant replied, "It is my master." Rebecca covered herself with her veil and met Isaac, who took her into his mother Sarah's tent. He loved Rebecca and married her.

Abraham took another wife and fathered six sons, who also had children of their own. But Abraham gave gifts to his other sons and sent them all away from Isaac and Rebecca and then gave everything he owned to Isaac. Abraham lived 175 years and died. And his sons Isaac and Ishmael buried him in Sarah's tomb in Canaan.

The Questions

- Why did Abraham insist on paying for a deed though he believed God had promised him all the land?
- Why did Abraham insist on Isaac choosing a wife from his own family and not a Canaanite woman? What had Abraham come to believe about God's covenant with him?
- Before Abraham died, why did Abraham give gifts to his other sons and send them away? What did this reveal about Abraham's growing understanding about God's covenant with him?
- Which promises within the covenant had been fulfilled when Abraham died? Had the covenant failed?

The Scripture Memory: Heb 11:13

The Hook Question

Which promises of God do I have faith will be fulfilled after and not before my death?

OT 8: Abraham's Family Lacked Integrity

The Misconceptions

- God uses only people of integrity and compassion to accomplish his plans.
- God adjusts his plans according to the decisions or responses of people.
- Being a victim of deceit or not experiencing blessings is always a sign of God's displeasure.

The Passages: Gen 25:19–34; 27:1—30:24; 35:16

The Main Parts

1. Abraham fathered two sons, Ishmael and Isaac.
2. God created twin boys, antagonists from in the womb, but God chose Jacob, the younger.
3. Jacob, through craft and deceit, twice received the better blessing.

The Story

Abraham fathered his first two sons: Ishmael with Hagar, then Isaac with Sarah. God promised to bless both sons, but before Isaac was born, God had chosen Isaac to be the heir of his covenant promise of land and a nation to Abraham. So, Abraham sent Ishmael away to build his own nation through his Egyptian wife.

But Isaac's wife, Rebecca, remained barren for many years until pregnant with twins. The twins fought within her womb, but God explained that these twins would become two nations. Once again, God chose before their birth that the firstborn son would serve the younger. The firstborn was named Esau, and his brother was named Jacob.

One day, Jacob was cooking stew. Esau was hungry, so he asked Jacob for some of the stew. Jacob agreed to give him stew if he traded his birthright to him, which Esau did.

Many years later, Isaac—now blind—was dying. Jacob entered his room but disguised as Esau to receive his father's last blessing as the firstborn. Isaac, believing Jacob was Esau, blessed Jacob, that he would master his brother and that nations would bow to him. After Jacob left, Esau entered Isaac's room to receive his expected blessing as the firstborn. That's when Isaac and Esau realized Jacob's deception of them. Esau was so angry, he vowed to kill Jacob as soon as Isaac died. Rebekah warned Jacob to escape to her brother Laban's home in Canaan, which Jacob did.

While living at Laban's, Jacob fell in love with Laban's younger daughter, Rachel, and asked to marry her. Laban required Jacob to work seven years to marry Rachel. But on the wedding night, Laban deceived Jacob by substituting Rachel's older sister, Leah, whom Jacob did not love. Jacob didn't discover the deception until the morning after the wedding. Laban allowed Rachel to marry Jacob after the wedding week but required another seven years of work. Leah quickly bore six sons, but Rachel was barren a long time before God gave her two sons. Rachel and Leah were so jealous and competitive of each other that they gave their personal maids to Jacob to each father two children on their own behalf. Rachel died while delivering her second son, but Jacob now had twelve sons, and each son became a tribe.

The Questions

- How many events in this story included deception?
- How did God resolve the conflicts according to his purpose in fulfilling his promises to Abraham?
- When deceptions or betrayal happen, does it affect God's planning or your expectations?

The Scripture Memory: Rom 8:28

The Hook Question

Can a deception from another person or another authority change God's plans for me?

OT 9: Joseph Trusted despite Being Imprisoned

The Misconceptions

- Negative or positive events in our lives are due to fate.
- Deceitful or evil actions against us must be defeated or overcome by our own actions.
- Evil intentions against us always end in evil results.

The Passage: Gen 37–47

The Major Parts

1. Family was jealous of Joseph, and Joseph was sold into slavery in Egypt by his brothers.
2. Joseph was successful and promoted in Potiphar's house, the prison, and Pharaoh's administration.
3. Family was brought to Egypt to be preserved through famine, where Abraham's sons grew in number.

The Story

Joseph was Jacob's second youngest son, but the first son of Jacob's most-loved wife, Rachel. Jacob loved Joseph more than his other sons and gave him a beautiful robe. His brothers became jealous. Joseph made them angrier when he spoke of two dreams he had had in which his brothers and parents bowed to him.

One morning, Jacob sent Joseph to join his brothers shepherding their flocks. His brothers recognized him coming because of his robe, and they planned how to kill him. Reuben, the oldest son, convinced them not to shed innocent blood. But while Reuben was away, the brothers sold Joseph to slave traders going to Egypt. They kept his robe, dipped it in goat's blood, and gave it to Jacob, so he would assume his son had been eaten by a wild animal.

The traders sold Joseph to Potiphar, the captain of the guard in Egypt. God honored Joseph, and he was promoted to rule over Potiphar's house. But Potiphar's wife tried to seduce Joseph many times and finally grabbed his cloak as he ran from her. She claimed Joseph had tried to seduce her, and Joseph was put in prison.

God honored Joseph, and he was promoted to oversee many prisoners. Two new prisoners, Pharaoh's cupbearer and baker, were assigned to him. One night, both prisoners had dreams they couldn't interpret. But Joseph interpreted them, saying in three days the baker would be hanged but the cupbearer would be released. Joseph's interpretation came true, and Joseph asked the cupbearer to remember him and his situation to Pharaoh.

But the cupbearer forgot about Joseph for two years until Pharaoh had a dream he couldn't interpret and the cupbearer remembered Joseph and suggested him to Pharaoh. Joseph interpreted the dream, saying there would be great harvests of grain for seven years, followed by seven years of famine. Joseph recommended storing the abundant harvests in preparation for the famine. God honored Joseph again, and he was promoted to second in authority only to Pharaoh. Joseph was appointed to manage all of Egypt's food storage. The news of available food reached Jacob and his sons, who were suffering from the famine in Canaan. Jacob sent his sons, except Benjamin, the last son of Rachel, to buy food in Egypt.

When the sons arrived in Egypt, they didn't recognize their brother Joseph. But Joseph recognized them and revealed himself to them. They bought food from him and Joseph forgave them, saying, "It was not you who sent me here, but God to preserve for you a remnant on earth and to save your lives by a great deliverance." And, because of Joseph, seventy members of Abraham's family were permitted to move to the Egyptian land of Goshen. They survived the famine and grew to be a very large family over the next 430 years they remained in Egypt.

The Questions

1. How do you think Joseph kept hope despite experiencing deception and betrayal? Where was his trust?
2. When do you think Joseph had insight into God's plans for good despite all the evil directed against him? How does that affect your view of others' evil intentions to you?
3. How are Joseph's responses different from other's typical responses?

The Scripture Memory: Gen 45:8

The Hook Question

What tests my faith about God's promises when I am wronged or disappointed from events that work against my best efforts?

OT 10: Moses Led the Exodus from Egypt

The Misconceptions

- Ease of labor is more important than freedom of worship.
- Divine promises become irrelevant and forgotten over generations.
- Seeing or experiencing a miracle will convince one to believe in God's promises.

The Passage: Exod 1:1—14:31

The Main Parts

1. The growth and persecution of the Israelites
2. The calling of Moses
3. The plagues, the exodus, and the parting of the sea

The Story

When famine struck Abraham's family of seventy, they went to Egypt for food. After 430 years, the Israelites grew to 600,000, and their size threatened the Egyptians, so Pharaoh made them slaves and commanded all male Israelites to be killed immediately after birth. But one Israelite mother hid her newborn son, then put him in a basket among river reeds where Pharaoh's daughter found him and named him Moses. Unknowingly, she hired Moses's mother to care for and nurse Moses. So Moses grew in Pharaoh's court, but he knew the secret of his heritage.

One day, Moses saw an Egyptian guard beat an Israelite slave to death. Moses killed the guard in retaliation. Moses learned there were witnesses, so he fled to the desert and became a shepherd. One day on a mountain called Sinai, he saw a bush on fire but not consumed. God spoke from the burning bush and told him to return to Egypt, confront Pharaoh, and demand the release of the Israelites from their slavery so they could worship God on Mount Sinai.

Pharaoh commanded Moses to prove his authority by performing a miracle. Moses threw his wooden staff to the ground, and it became a serpent. Pharaoh commanded his magicians to do the same thing, which they did, but Moses's serpent swallowed the other serpents. Pharaoh refused Moses, so Moses commanded the Nile River turn to blood. Again, the magicians did the same, and Pharaoh again refused Moses. Moses warned of a plague of frogs, but the magicians did the same, and Pharaoh again refused. Moses announced a plague of gnats, but the magicians could not imitate gnats and told Pharaoh this was the hand of God. But Pharaoh again refused Moses. After each plague, Pharaoh made harsher demands on the Israelites, so the Israelites turned against Moses. Moses announced a tenth plague, that the firstborn males of all Egyptians and all cattle would die in one night. But the Lord would pass over every house where the blood of a lamb was put over the doorway. Moses directed the Israelites to remain in their houses, eat a meal while the Lord passed over, and pack to prepare to leave quickly. Pharaoh's firstborn son was among those who died, and Pharaoh commanded Moses and the Israelites to leave.

They left Egypt by following God, who used a pillar of cloud by day and a pillar of fire by night to lead them. But shortly after the Israelites left, Pharaoh ordered his army to bring them back. When the Egyptian army caught up to them, they were at the shore of the Red Sea with no path of escape. The pillar of fire moved between the Egyptians and the Israelites for protection, and a wind pushed the sea and opened a dry path to the other side. The Israelites safely crossed the sea on a dry path, and the pillar moved, permitting the Egyptian army to follow after the Israelites. But then the waters immediately closed over the army and they all drowned, and the Israelites continued their journey to worship God at the mountain.

The Questions

1. What reveals the level of interest of the Israelites in expecting God's fulfillment of his covenant promises? What discouragements affect our level of expectation today?
2. Does God's judgment of the injustices of the Egyptians warn or encourage you?
3. Which qualities of Moses's courage impressed you?

The Scripture Memory: Exod 14:31

The Hook Questions

Do I need to see a miracle to believe God's promises?

Would I respond differently than Pharaoh did?

OT 11: God Provided for Israel's Needs

The Misconceptions

- God is concerned only about people's spiritual lives, leaving them to satisfy their own physical needs.
- God's frustrations with man's constant grumbling produces only discipline and judgment.
- God's laws are burdensome and demanding, because God is a stern King.

The Passages: Exod 15:27—17:14; 19:1—20:21; 32:1-35

The Main Parts

1. Miracles: Provision of water through wood, food, manna, water through rock; victory over Amalekites
2. God's presence at Mount Sinai
3. God commissions the nation to be his priesthood, reflecting God's glory and character

The Story

Three days after Moses led the Israelites from Egypt into the desert, they had little water remaining and natural water was bitter. The people grumbled to Moses. Moses prayed to God, who directed Moses to throw wood in the water. The water became sweet and refreshed them enough to continue to an oasis of twelve springs, where they rested.

Six weeks after leaving Egypt, the people again grumbled to Moses that they had little food remaining and would have been better off if they had remained in Egypt. Moses prayed to God, who sent quail to the people at twilight. And then, every morning after that, except on the Sabbath, a wafer-like bread, which they named manna, would fall from heaven like dew, for them to collect and eat throughout the day. They couldn't keep it overnight because it would be filled by maggots by morning except on the night before Sabbath. Keeping it overnight would enable them to avoid harvesting on the Sabbath.

As they continued on their journey, they again grumbled to Moses that they had little water. And Moses told God, who told Moses to hit a rock with his staff. Enough water gushed out of the rock for them to satisfy their thirst and continue their journey.

Israel traveled rapidly, but those who were slower and followed behind the main group were attacked by the Amalekites. Moses directed his general, Joshua, to fight against them while Moses stood on a mountain, held his staff up, and called on God. When Moses prayed like that, the Israelites would win, but if his arms lowered, they would lose. So Moses's brother Aaron and another kept his arms raised until they eventually defeated the Amalekites. God directed Moses to write about their attacks to justify destroying all the Amalekites later.

Three months after leaving Egypt, they finally arrived at Mount Sinai. God's presence was obvious with thunder, lightning, and a thick cloud covering the mountain. God spoke from the mountain, calling on them to acknowledge that his miracles had brought release from Egypt and provided for them during their travel. God wanted to establish an agreement, or covenant, with them that included commandments for them to obey. He would choose them as a kingdom of his priests, and they would be set aside to be his people by agreeing to his laws, because they reflected his glory and character. To refuse to obey his commands would dishonor God

The Questions

1. Why did the Israelites complain as if each issue for food and water was unknown to God?
2. What does God's response to each Israelite complaint reveal about his character?
3. Do you think the Israelites were surprised by God's responses to their grumbling, or were they expecting his solutions?
4. Why does God care so personally about seeing his laws are being obeyed?

The Scripture Memory: Rom 2:10–11

The Hook Question

Which past responses from God have affected how I trust or expect God to respond to me in the future?

OT 12: Aaron and Miriam Dishonored Moses

The Misconceptions

- All those who lead have equal authority.
- Leaders evaluate other leaders according to their own personal standards or motivations.
- Leaders assume their leadership position because of their self-appointment.

The Passage: Num 12:1–16

The Main Parts

1. Miriam questioned Aaron about Moses's leadership because God had also spoken to them.
2. God met Miriam, Aaron, and Moses to explain why he had chosen Moses and to express his anger with them
3. God punished Miriam with leprosy and had her remain outside the camp in shame for one week.

The Story

Moses was leading 600,000 people who were grumbling for water and food, traveling through the desert, and was miserable answering the many grumbles and complaints of so many people. Moses had an older sister, Miriam, who asked their other brother, Aaron, "Has the Lord spoken only through Moses? Hasn't he also spoken through us?" Now the Lord heard this and asked Moses, Aaron, and Miriam to meet him in front of the tent of meeting, called the tabernacle, where God met with Israel's leadership and the priests. There the Lord came down in a pillar of cloud and told Miriam and Aaron to come forward.

The Lord said, "When a prophet is among you, I will reveal myself to him in visions and dreams. But that is not true of my servant, Moses. He is faithful in all my house, and with him I speak face-to-face, clearly and not in riddles. So why weren't you afraid to speak against my servant Moses?" The Lord was very angry with them, and he left them.

When the Lord's cloud rose above the tabernacle, they saw Miriam's skin was now white with leprosy. Aaron called to Moses, confessed their sin, and asked Moses to ask the Lord for healing, which Moses did. The

Lord replied that if Miriam's father had spit in her face, she would have been disgraced for seven days outside the camp before being allowed to return. Therefore, Miriam should be sent outside the camp for seven days before returning. So the Israelites stayed where they were for seven days until Miriam could reenter their camp.

The Questions

1. Why do you think Miriam and Aaron weren't afraid to speak against Moses?
2. Do you think they were questioning Moses's leadership or their own positions as leaders?
3. Which criteria were Miriam and Aaron using to criticize Moses?
4. Why did God respond quickly when hearing influential leaders speak critically of Moses's leadership?
5. Which character in Moses caused God to appoint and support Moses as leader?

The Scripture Memory: Num 12:8; Heb 13:17

The Hook Question

How can I hold religious leadership accountable without speaking against them to others?

OT 13: Israel Dishonored God at Mount Sinai

The Misconceptions:
- Man remains faithful to his promises.
- God forgives all sin without anger or consequences.

The Passage: Exod 19:1—32:35

The Main Parts
1. God called Israel to represent and serve him before all the nations.
2. God gave laws to govern society and to fulfill how he wanted to be worshiped.
3. The Israelites committed idolatry as soon as Moses wasn't with them.
4. The Israelites who objected to obeying Moses were killed.

The Story

As the Israelites camped at Mount Sinai, God told Moses that Israel, as his priests, must fully obey him. After Israel consecrated and purified themselves for three days, God called Moses and his brother, Aaron, to join him on the mountain to be taught by God. Moses returned to repeat God's commands to Israel as part of Israel's covenant with God. The people agreed to these laws and said, "Everything the Lord has said we will do."

Moses returned again to the mountain with his general, Joshua, but Aaron remained with the people. Moses and Joshua waited six days before God called Moses to continue alone in the cloud for forty days and nights.

While Moses was gone, the Israelites asked Aaron to make gods to lead them, arguing that Moses was gone and no one knew what had happened to him. The people collected their gold jewelry and gave it to Aaron to make a golden calf idol and then announced this idol was the god that brought them out of Egypt. Aaron made an altar in front of the calf and announced a festival for the next day.

God knew the Israelites had turned from him and considered destroying all the Israelites and beginning another nation from Moses's descendants. Moses argued that God's honor would be damaged and the other nations would believe God had always intended to kill them. Moses also reminded God of his promise to Abram of descendants who would be as many as the stars. So God did not destroy all the people.

Moses offered the Israelites the opportunity to follow him as their leader as he followed the Lord. But three thousand people chose against following Moses, and they were killed by the priestly tribe of Levi. Then God sent a plague to punish those who sinned against him and warned he still might decide to punish them. But God gave orders for Moses to continue to the land that he had promised Abraham, Isaac, and Jacob.

The Questions

1. Why could Israel turn so quickly to idolatry after having seen all of God's miracles firsthand?
2. Was the death of three thousand Israelites necessary for purification or because of God's anger and desire to punish?
3. What was God's plan for the people? Was the plan affected by the people's unfaithfulness?

The Scripture Memory: Exod 20:24b

The Hook Questions

Have I ever offered a promise to God even as I questioned my ability to keep it? Why?

Has God ever broken a promise to me?

OT 14: God Established the Sacrificial System

The Misconceptions

- Offering sacrifices to God earns his favor.
- God requires sacrifices as a dutiful requirement.
- Sacrifices to God influence God's willingness to bless his people.
- Sacrifices are all the same and serve the same purpose.

The Passages: Lev 1–7, 16; Ps 51:16–17

The Main Parts

1. The purposes of sacrifice
2. The procedures for sacrifice
3. The nature of the sacrifice
4. Bad examples of sacrifice

The Story

While at Mount Sinai, God taught Moses how he desired the people to thank and honor him and how to restore their relationship to him after dishonoring and disobeying him. They were to use sacrifices that would represent the guilty person. Some sacrifices were offered by individuals, and other sacrifices were offered by the entire nation.

Some sacrifices were offered to bring pleasure to God or were a part of national feast celebrations to remember God's acts in their history. Some sacrifices were to express thankfulness to God or the community. Some sacrifices were guilt or sin offerings to provide a substitute death in place of the person or the nation, which permitted God's anger and wrath to be poured out on the sacrifice instead of on the worshipper. The worshipper had to prove personal ownership of the substitute offering and put his hands on the head of the offering to personally identify with the substitute sacrifice.

God gave detailed commands on how the priests were to examine an offering to ensure it was a perfect substitution. God commanded that no fat or blood should be eaten by the priests, because the life of the offering belonged to God and the blood represented that life. God directed what the priests were to wear and even how to wash their clothes after offering sacrifices.

But years later, priests would often become corrupted and keep the sacrifices to eat for themselves. God would then cleanse and discipline the priesthood, sometimes at the cost of the priests' own lives.

The Questions

- How did God reveal that sacrifice was important to him?
- What's the difference between using sacrifices to substitute for the penalty required and using sacrifices to earn something from God?
- Do you offer any sacrifices to God, and for what purposes do you offer them?

The Scripture Memory: Rom 12:1

The Hook Question

How do my sacrifices to God reveal I am honestly honoring God and trying to reestablish my relationship with God instead of trying to earn something from God?

OT 15: The Spies Refused God's Promised Land

The Misconceptions

- The power of nations or kingdoms, not God, determine the nations' or kingdoms' own homelands.
- An entire nation does not bear the consequences of a few, nonelected leaders.
- God judges and disciplines only national leaders but not an entire nation.

The Passage: Num 13:1—14:45

The Main Points

1. God unconditionally promised Abraham the land of Canaan and then chose his descendants to be his nation of priests in the land.
2. Ten spies reported they couldn't beat the people already living in the land.
3. God's judgment on unbelief and the reward of the promised land.

The Story

God commanded Abram to go to an unfamiliar land. When Abram entered the land of Canaan, God promised Abram, "I will give this land to your descendants," and confirmed his promises to Abram with an unconditional covenant.

But Abraham's descendants left Canaan for Egypt for 430 years. God, however, delivered Israel from Egypt and led them back to Canaan's border. God directed Moses to choose men to spy out Canaan. For forty days, twelve spies from the twelve tribes of Israel spied out Canaan and the fruitfulness of the land.

When the spies returned, they all agreed the land was fruitful. But ten of the spies said Canaan was filled with powerful warriors who would defeat them and persuaded Israel to return to Egypt instead. Two of the spies, Joshua and Caleb, believed in God's promises and disagreed, saying, "But the Lord is with us! Do not be afraid of them." But the people threatened to kill both of them.

God was angry with Israel and told Moses, "How long will they refuse to believe in me despite all the miracles I've performed? I will strike them down with a plague and destroy them and make you into a strong nation." But Moses replied, as he had earlier at Mount Sinai, that the nations would say God was not powerful enough to bring the people into the land. God again relented but promised that the entire generation over twenty years old would die in the desert over the next forty years.

When the Israelites heard God's judgment, they changed their minds and decided to attack the Canaanite tribes despite Moses's warning that the Lord would not be with them. But they ignored Moses's warning, attacked the tribes, and were killed by the Canaanites. So the rest of the generation wandered in the wilderness for forty years until they all died except for Caleb and Joshua.

The Questions

1. Did the Israelites or Canaanites do anything to either earn or lose the land? What was God's purpose in promising the land?
2. Which actions or attitudes of the Israelites dishonored God?
3. Is it ever too late to change a decision of unbelief to belief in God's promises?

The Scripture Memory: Num 14:24

The Hook Questions

Which promises of God do I distrust I will receive?

What must I do to change the consequences of my unbelief?

OT 16: Rahab Believed God's Promise at Jericho

The Misconceptions
- God uses only his chosen righteous ones to accomplish his plans.
- God uses only his written words (Scripture) to reveal himself.

The Passages: Deut 34:1–9; Josh 1:1—6:27

The Main Points
1. Spies meet Rahab the harlot.
2. The Israelites cross the parted Jordan River.
3. The Israelites destroy the city walls and protect Rahab.

The Story

After forty years in the wilderness and the deaths of the unbelieving generation, the Israelites were again at the border of Canaan. Moses had recently died and Joshua—one of the two spies who had recommended entering Canaan forty years earlier—now led them.

Joshua sent two spies to look over the land, particularly nearby Jericho. The spies secretly entered Jericho and hid in a prostitute's home that was part of the city wall. The woman, Rahab, told the spies she knew the Lord had given Jericho to Israel. Everyone knew the Lord had brought the Israelites through the Red Sea, and they had just killed two powerful kings of the nearby Amorite tribe. Finally, she told them she knew their Lord was the God of all heaven and earth. Because she had hid them, Rahab asked them to spare the lives of her and her family. The spies agreed and safely returned to Joshua.

The Jordan River at Jericho was at flood stage. God told Joshua to have the priests walk into the river with the ark of the covenant, a carved box containing artifacts of God's history with them. As soon as they stepped into the water, the water stopped upriver, so the riverbed became dry and all the Israelites walked across. When the last person crossed, the priests stepped out of the riverbed and the river returned to flood stage. The Israelites camped east of Jericho, celebrated the Passover, and ate their first food from their new land. The manna stopped appearing the day they ate the food in Canaan.

As Joshua scouted the land near Jericho alone, he saw a man in his path with a drawn sword. He asked the man if he was for them or their enemies. The man said, "Neither. I have come as commander of the army of God. Take off your shoes, for you are standing on holy ground." This commander, who was called the Lord, said he had delivered Jericho into Joshua's hand.

The Israelites marched around Jericho's walls, led by priests, then armed men, and then musicians blowing rams' horns. They marched like this for six straight days. On the seventh day, the trumpet blast lasted long, and the Israelites gave a loud shout and the city walls collapsed and the soldiers entered the city. Rahab and her family were preserved by the soldiers, but everyone else in Jericho was killed. Rahab remained with Israel, and centuries later, she appeared as one of four women in the ancestral genealogy of Jesus.

The Questions

1. What did Rahab say she believed about the Lord and the Israelites?
2. Since no Israelites had yet spoken to Rahab, how had she heard the stories of Israel? What does that reveal about the power of stories and any special training to be a storyteller?
3. Why would the attacking Israelites lead with priests and not with warriors?

The Scripture Memory: Josh 2:11

The Hook Questions

Am I unqualified to repeat biblical stories?

What must I do before being qualified?

OT 17: The Israelites Were Defeated at Ai

The Misconceptions

- Personal sins affect only the person who sinned; others do not bear the consequences.
- The causes of calamity and fear of even worse events can be resolved only by man.

The Passage: Josh 7:1—8:35

The Main Points

1. Achan's theft of what belonged to God led to Israel's defeat.
2. Joshua mourned their defeat until the Lord explained the cause and resolution.
3. Achan was killed; the Israelites attacked the enemy victoriously and recommitted to the covenant.

The Story

When the Israelites miraculously defeated Jericho, all the silver, gold, and metal treasures were to be given to the Lord. But Achan of the tribe of Judah saw treasure he wanted to keep for himself and hid some silver and gold and a beautiful Babylonian robe in his tent rather than offering it to the Lord.

Joshua was confident following their victory over Jericho, so he sent spies to plan how to conquer the nearby city of Ai. The spies returned, suggesting only a small detachment of three thousand soldiers would be necessary, which is all Joshua sent. But the detachment was easily defeated, and the Israelites ran from the enemy's army.

Joshua reacted by tearing his clothes and pouring dust on his head. He told his elders to do the same for an entire day. Joshua feared he would be rejected as general and no one would listen to him again. He believed the defeat would encourage other enemies to defeat them and damage God's reputation. He regretted they had entered Canaan and feared the Lord had brought them into Canaan to die.

But the Lord told Joshua the reason for the defeat. Israel had sinned and violated the covenant. They had stolen what was to be given to the Lord and kept it hidden. And they were all responsible for the sin until they removed the evil from them.

The Lord told Joshua to assemble all the tribes before the Lord, who identified Judah as the guilty tribe. Then the clans of Judah were assembled, and the Lord identified the guilty clan. Then the families of the clan were assembled, and the guilty family was identified. Then, one by one, the men of the family were presented until Achan was identified. Joshua confronted him, and Achan admitted his thievery. Joshua's men went to his tent and gathered the silver, gold, and robe he had kept from the Lord. Then the people took Achan, his family, cattle, tent, and all his belongings and stoned them and burned everything and covered it all with rocks.

With the evil removed from their midst, God told Joshua to be courageous and attack Ai again, and this time, they could keep their plunder. Joshua took thirty thousand warriors, and they attacked Ai, killing all the inhabitants, and then burned the city to the ground.

Then Joshua built an altar on Mount Ebal, and they offered many sacrifices to God, and Joshua had the blessings and the curses of the law of Moses read to all the people.

The Questions

1. Where did Achan fail in his thinking that he could cover his theft?
2. Why do you think the Lord went through the long process of narrowing the identification of Achan? What do you think was going through Achan's mind during the process?
3. Which benefits were there for the Lord in holding all the Israelites accountable for Achan's sin?
4. For what purposes did all the Israelites participate in the death of Achan and his family?
5. Joshua sent three thousand for the first attack on Ai but sent thirty thousand on the second attack. What had he learned?

The Scripture Memory: Rev 3:19

The Hook Question

Is there anything I am keeping for myself that rightfully belongs to God?

OT 18: Israel Was Deceived before Defeating Kings

The Misconceptions

- Our own knowledge provides sufficient understanding to make wise decisions.
- Our small and often irrelevant personal acts and attitudes are unnoticed by God.
- God's attention is focused only on the large, consequential acts that fulfill his plans.

The Passage: Josh 9:1—10:43

The Main Points

1. The deception of the Gibeonites and the failure of the Israelites to consult God
2. The five-king alliance attacked the Gibeonites, who called on Joshua for protection
3. Joshua's army marched all night, killed the kings and the armies, and controlled the south.

The Story

God commanded Israel not to marry or make treaties with foreign tribes, because it could lead to their worshipping pagan gods and abandoning worship of the true God. However, a few months after Israel's victories over Jericho and Ai, the Gibeonite tribe, with four cities near the Israelites, wanted to avoid the same disastrous results, so they sent representatives to make a treaty with Israel.

The representatives cleverly disguised themselves to appear as if they had come from a great distance beyond Canaan—even bringing dry and moldy bread they claimed was fresh when they began their trip. They brought old cracked wineskins, and their clothes and sandals appeared to be worn out. The Israelites initially questioned signing a treaty because they were suspicious they might be nearby enemies, but the Gibeonites said they would be servants of the Israelites and pointed again to their evidence of long travel. Joshua and the Israelites agreed to a peace treaty approved by Israel's leaders. But they failed to ask the Lord for his guidance and blessing.

Three days after signing the treaty, the Israelites discovered the Gibeonites truly did live nearby, so they marched to the Gibeonites' four cities. But they did not attack them because of their treaty. Israel's leaders knew if they violated their oath, the Lord would discipline them. If they honored their treaty and spared them, the Gibeonites would be their servants. But Israel wouldn't be protected from Gibeon's idolatries.

Joshua told the Gibeonites that, because of their deception, they were now under a curse and would always be woodcutters and water carriers for the community and the house of God. The Gibeonites replied how fearful they had been, because they knew God had promised the Israelites the whole land and all the inhabitants would be killed. Though they were now servants of the Israelites, their lives were spared.

Knowing of the Israelites' victories over Jericho and Ai and their treaty with the Gibeonites, five Amorite kings allied together to attack Gibeah. The Gibeonites sent a report to Joshua, and Joshua marched his army all night to honor their treaty. They attacked and killed the five kings and their armies, enabling them to divide the northern and southern lands of Canaan, which resulted in conquering all of Canaan.

The Questions

1. Why couldn't the Israelites ignore the treaty if the Gibeonites had entered into it fraudulently?
2. How did God use the treaty to accomplish his purposes for Israel?
3. Which dangers to Israel remained because of the treaty?

The Scripture Memory: Rom 8:28

The Hook Questions

Does anyone come to mind who I think deceived me in the past?

How would my thoughts about that person affect my ability to reflect the glory of God in my life to that person?

OT 19: Reluctant Gideon Defeated the Midianites

Misconceptions:

- God is intolerant of our lack of faith.
- God calls only faith-filled people to lead in times of crisis.

Passage: Judg 6–7

Main Points

1. The cycle of idolatrous rebellion, crying to God to end their oppression, God sending a judge
2. Gideon's disbelief in God's call of being the deliverer and proving of God
3. Gideon's victory and deliverance from oppression through God

The Story

God commanded Israel to defeat all the foreign tribes in Canaan to avoid being tempted by their false idolatry. But Israel failed to defeat them and Israel soon turned to worship their idols. The Canaanite tribes would oppress Israel, who would pray for deliverance, and God would raise up a warrior judge to deliver them—until they became idolatrous again. God also sent prophets to identify Israel's sin and communicate God's sadness over them.

One time when the Midianites were oppressing Israel, an Israelite, Gideon, was hiding threshed wheat from the Midianites in the bottom of a winepress. That's where the angel of the Lord found him and said, "The Lord is with you, mighty warrior!" Gideon replied, "But the Lord abandoned us, and we're oppressed." The Lord said, "I am sending you to rescue Israel from the Midianites!" Gideon argued that his family was the weakest among all the Israelites, and he was the least in his family. The Lord replied that he would be with Gideon. Gideon asked for a sign that the angel was the Lord, and Gideon brought an offering. The angel touched it with his staff, causing the rock to flame and burn the offering as the angel of the Lord disappeared.

That night the Lord told Gideon to destroy his father's altars to the Midianite gods. Gideon burned the wooden idols to sacrifice one of his father's bulls to the Lord. When the townspeople saw what he had done, they demanded Gideon's father kill Gideon, but his father said, "If this idol is god, then let this god defend himself."

But Gideon wanted another sign the Lord would provide victory and asked the Lord to have dew fall on a lambskin fleece but not on the surrounding ground. The Lord performed that sign, but Gideon asked for another sign by making the surrounding ground wet but the fleece remain dry. And the Lord did that too.

The next day, 32,000 men answered Gideon's call to fight the 135,000 Midianites. Gideon released any who were afraid, and all but 10,000 left him. But the Lord told Gideon he still had too many men and directed Gideon to go to the stream to drink water and dismiss those who drank while kneeling. Only 300 brought water to their mouths in cupped hands, revealing their constant alertness to danger, and Gideon sent the rest home.

That night, the Lord told Gideon to take the 300 men near the Midianite camp. Gideon divided his men into three companies, each with a trumpet in one hand and holding a lamp covered by a jar in the other. At Gideon's signal, they broke their jars, and the torches appeared to surround the camp. They blew their trumpets that so confused and terrified the Midianites, they fought themselves and fled in every direction, giving the victory.

The Israelites asked Gideon to rule over them. Gideon required each person to give him a gold ring from the plunder, totaling about forty-three pounds, which he made into an ephod, or religious breastplate. The Israelites had peace for forty years, but then they still violated their commitment to the Lord by turning to worship the ephod.

The Questions

1. Which examples reveal Gideon's lack of faith in himself? How did his faith in God grow?
2. Which examples reveal God's evaluation of who has an advantage at critical times?
3. Did you feel disappointment with Israel's worship of the ephod? Having heard of God's responses to Israel in the story, how do you think God would respond to such disappointment?

The Scripture Memory: Zech 4:6

The Hook Question

What has God previously provided me that increased my faith to trust for something even greater from him?

OT 20: Israel Rejected God and Asked for a King

The Misconceptions

- Influential fathers should appoint their children to continue their legacy, even if unqualified or unfit.
- Children of respected ruling leaders will faithfully continue their parents' honorable leadership.

The Passage: 1 Sam 2:11—10:1

The Main Points

1. Eli and immoral sons
2. Capture of ark
3. Samuel and immoral sons
4. Call of people for a king

The Story

Eli was the high priest serving at the tabernacle. He had two sons, Hophni and Phineas, who dishonored God by taking the best parts of the worshippers' sacrifices for themselves and being immoral with women at the door to the tabernacle. Their behavior was well known and reported to Eli, who scolded them but did nothing. Finally, God warned Eli through a young boy named Samuel who served in the tabernacle. Samuel warned Eli that he and his sons would die and God would raise up a new priest from a different line, ending Eli's priestly line.

During this time, the Philistines fought against Israel. Hophni and Phineas took the ark of the covenant to the battle front lines, thinking God's presence and power through the ark would bring victory. But the Philistines killed Hophni and Phineas, captured the ark, and took it to one of their cities. When Eli was told this, he fell over backwards, broke his neck, and died.

When Samuel grew older, he became a respected prophet and judge. He also had two sons he appointed to be judges over Israel. But, like Eli's sons, they were dishonest, took bribes, perverted justice, and didn't follow their father. The people complained about Samuel's sons, and instead of judges, they asked Samuel to give them a king like other nations, to lead them into battles.

Samuel believed they were rejecting his own leadership and legacy, but God said they were really rejecting God as king. God told Samuel to warn them what would happen with a king. A king would place heavy taxes on the people, gather their sons into his army and their daughters as perfumers and cooks, take their best cattle for himself, and make the people his slaves. But the people still asked for a king to lead them and fight their battles. So God told Samuel to listen to them and give them a king. And God directed Samuel to anoint Saul, who was thirty years old when he became king.

The Questions

- Why did Eli and Samuel want their sons to assume the roles they held? What should they have done before appointing their sons to their positions?
- Why would Eli and Samuel ignore the feedback they received about their sons from the local people?
- What was the motivation for the people to reject the warnings of God and still ask for a king?

The Scripture Memory: Lev 19:2

The Hook Questions

Have examples of church leadership being wrongly influenced by the culture affected my perspective toward the church? Why?

OT 21: God Rejected Saul as King

The Misconceptions

- God's call to offer sacrifices is our greatest measure of devotion.
- God doesn't keep track of offenses against his people forever.

The Passage: 1 Sam 15

The Main Points

1. Amalekites' attack on Israelites and God's judgment
2. God's call through Samuel to erase memory of Amalekites
3. Saul's decision to offer sacrifices from people instead of to obey
4. Samuel's announcement of rejection of kingship and his killing of Agag

The Story

When Israel left Egypt for Canaan, some families were exhausted and fell behind, where Amalekite tribesmen attacked them. God told Moses to record the attacks to remind Joshua in the future that God promised to erase the memory of the Amalekites, who killed the weary, because these Amalekites didn't fear God.

Years later, God directed the prophet Samuel to tell King Saul the time had come to completely destroy the Amalekites and everything that belonged to them. They were not to spare anyone but put every man, woman, child, infant, and their cattle, sheep, camels, and donkeys to death. Saul's men destroyed everything that was despised and weak, but they spared the Amalekite king and the best of their sheep, cattle, and fat lambs.

God told Samuel he regretted making Saul king because Saul had turned from him and no longer obeyed his instructions. So God rejected Saul as king. God directed Samuel to tell Saul that God was taking the kingdom from him. But as soon as Saul saw Samuel coming, Saul said, "The Lord bless you! I have carried out the Lord's instructions."

But Samuel answered, "Then why do I still hear lambs and cattle?"

Saul answered, "The soldiers brought the best to sacrifice to the Lord and destroyed all the rest."

Samuel yelled, "Stop! Let me tell you what the Lord said to me last night! You were once small in your own eyes, but God anointed you king.

He directed you to completely destroy the wicked Amalekites, but you didn't obey. Why did you save the plunder and do evil?"

Saul answered, "But I did obey the Lord. I completely destroyed the Amalekites and brought back their king. The soldiers took sheep and cattle from the plunder to sacrifice them to the Lord your God."

Samuel asked, "Does the Lord delight in burnt offerings and sacrifices as much as in obeying him? To obey is better than sacrifice, and to obey is better than the fat of sacrificed rams. Because you rejected the word of the Lord, he has rejected you as king."

Saul said, "I have sinned. I violated the Lord's command and your instructions. I was afraid of the people, so I gave in to them. Now I beg you, forgive my sin and come back with me, so that I may worship the Lord."

But Samuel answered, "I will not go back with you. You rejected the word of the Lord, and the Lord has rejected you as king." Then Samuel commanded that the king of the Amalekites be brought to him. And Samuel killed the Amalekite king and left Saul. Samuel never saw Saul again, though he mourned over him.

The Questions

1. Why do you think Saul took so long to finally admit his disobedience?
2. What does God reveal about his character and justice that he would demand vengeance hundreds of years later after the Amalekites' forefathers had attacked the weak Israelites during the exodus?
3. What were Saul's motivations or expectations for offering sacrifices even when offered by himself in disobedience?

The Scripture Memory: 1 Sam 15:22

The Hook Questions

Will God think better of me because of the sacrifices I have offered to him?

What do I believe influences God to think better of me?

OT 22: David Anointed as King

The Misconceptions

- God's leadership appointments always have his blessings and are unchanging.
- Confidence in God's calling still requires personal strategy to achieve the call.
- Every strategic benefit that comes to you should be pursued without regard to other influences.

The Passages: 1 Sam 16:13; 24:1–23; 2 Sam 1:1—5:5

The Main Points

1. Samuel anointed David while Saul was still king.
2. Saul had an evil spirit, became jealous of David, and tried to kill him.
3. David was in exile, and Saul was killed in battle.
4. Israel anointed David as their king, joining with Judah and uniting the kingdom.

The Story

After the prophet Samuel told King Saul that God had torn the kingdom from him, God next sent Samuel to Bethlehem to anoint David as the next king. Though Saul remained on the throne, God's Spirit left Saul, and an evil spirit tormented him instead, and David was brought into the court to play his harp to bring relief to Saul.

David also served as Saul's armor-bearer and became a successful and popular warrior, which made Saul jealous of him. During one of Saul's furious rages, Saul tried to kill David, so David fled from him and sought refuge under a Philistine king. David recruited six hundred men, who raided other Philistine cities but left no survivors to report who had attacked them.

Though Saul chased David with his army to kill him, David had two strategic opportunities to kill Saul. But David refused to take advantage of those opportunities, because Saul still remained the anointed king, which David honored.

Saul was eventually killed in a battle against the Philistines. Saul's general, Abner, installed Saul's son as the new king of Israel. But the tribe of

Judah had anointed David as their king. Abner and David's general, Joab, continued to fight each other to establish who would be king. Abner became angry with Saul's son, so he left Saul's son and joined David's army. But Abner's presence in the army angered Joab, because Abner had earlier killed Joab's brother. Against David's will, Joab avenged his brother's death by killing Abner. David sincerely mourned for Abner as he had for the death of Saul. David's attitude toward Saul and then Abner caused Israel to trust David and anoint him king over all the tribes of Israel, uniting Judah and Israel under David's kingship.

The Questions

1. David knew he was anointed to be king, so why didn't he kill Saul when he had strategic opportunities to assume his promised kingship? What more was he expecting from God before becoming king?
2. Instead of killing Saul and Saul's general, who were trying to kill him, he mourned their deaths. If he had instead celebrated their deaths as his victory and fulfillment of God's anointing, how would the choice of David as king by both Judah and Israel been different?
3. Which sincere, public demonstration of David's character brought peace and unity to two warring nations?

The Scripture Memory: Ps 18:3

The Hook Questions

How do I decide if an opportunity is from God or not?

How long should I wait for God to bring his promises to fulfillment without my own actions to remove any obstacles that appear to delay the promises?

OT 23: David's Unfaithfulness and Discipline

The Misconceptions

- Confidence from past victories ensures future successes.
- Private sins can be hidden from God and the public.
- Forgiveness of sins protects from future consequences of those sins.

The Passages: 2 Sam 6:13–19; 7:8–17; 8; 11:1–17; 12:15–18;15:13; 18:32–33; 1 Kgs 1

The Main Points

1. David loved God and was loved by God.
2. David committed adultery and murder.
3. Absalom and Adonijah were killed while attempting to take David's kingship.
4. David agreed to anoint his son Solomon to succeed him.

The Story

David began ruling Israel and Judah, committed to serving and loving God. He brought the ark of the covenant to Jerusalem in a great celebration with many sacrifices. He provided a banquet for everyone, and the people responded with shouts of celebration and worship. This brought great pleasure to God, who announced through a prophet that David's name would be great and that both his kingdom and Israel's promised homeland would be eternal. David became successful in building Jerusalem and other cities, became wealthy, and was victorious over all his enemies. He also wrote many worship hymns, or psalms, to God, and God blessed him.

However, when David got older, he began an adulterous affair with Bathsheba, the wife of a faithful soldier who was away fighting a battle for Israel. Bathsheba became pregnant, and David tried to hide the adultery, even giving orders that caused her husband's death in battle.

God sent the prophet Nathan to confront David about his sin. David immediately confessed and pleaded for forgiveness. Though forgiven, his sin brought several consequences. First, the son he had with Bathsheba died. Second, David's beloved son Absalom revolted against his father. David would not fight Absalom but fled as Absalom entered Jerusalem. But

David's general killed Absalom despite David's command not to harm him. David continued to war against those who rebelled but grew old and feeble, which encouraged his oldest remaining son, Adonijah, to be crowned king.

But David and Bathsheba had had a second son, Solomon, and David had promised Bathsheba that Solomon would follow him as king. So David called his trusted priest and leaders to anoint Solomon as king and to have the trumpets and leaders announce Solomon's kingship. Adonijah realized he now was a threat to Solomon and raced to hold on to the altar for refuge. But Solomon graciously allowed Adonijah to live as long as he made no attempts to overthrow Solomon as king.

The Questions

1. Why did David think he could hide his adultery and murder from an all-seeing God?
2. Though David confessed and was forgiven, which consequences of the sin still took place?
3. Which blessings and honor did David still retain though disciplined? Why do you think those privileges were not taken?

The Scripture Memory: Ps 51:1

The Hook Questions

Which sins or actions do I try to keep secret from God so I escape accountability and discipline?

Which misunderstanding about God do I have so I can delay confession and add good works or righteousness so God will eventually ignore my disobedience?

OT 24: Solomon Ruled with Wisdom but Failed

The Misconceptions

- The extent of sin's effects can be safely tested, controlled, and limited by man's choices.
- Wisdom is more valuable and powerful than obedience.

The Passages: 1 Kgs 3:1–15; 5:8–17; 8:22—9:9; 10:23; 11:1–43

The Main Points

1. Solomon asked God for wisdom to judge, and God gave him wisdom and added honor and riches.
2. Solomon built and dedicated the Jerusalem temple.
3. Solomon grew dissatisfied with wisdom, chose pleasure, and turned to doing evil.
4. God tore the kingdom from Solomon.

The Story

After King David died, God visited Solomon in a dream and asked what he most desired. Solomon answered, "Wisdom to provide justice." The answer pleased God, because Solomon didn't ask for riches and honor. So God also added riches and honor and a long life if Solomon would obey God's laws.

Solomon began his rule building his administration. Then he made an alliance with Pharaoh, king of Egypt, and married Pharaoh's daughter. He contracted with the king of Lebanon for wood and quarried stone to build a temple for God and a palace for himself.

Solomon dedicated the temple with prayers, asking that the temple be where all people could know that God would listen, and then Solomon offered sacrifices. The Lord appeared a second time to Solomon, again promising to answer Solomon's requests and to establish his throne if Solomon obeyed God's laws. But he also warned that, if he failed to obey, Israel would be removed from their homeland and God would reject the temple.

Solomon became greater in riches and wisdom than all the other kings of the earth. Kings and queens came to sit with Solomon and hear his wisdom. But then Solomon believed wisdom was meaningless and brought only grief and pain. So he explored pleasure and didn't deny himself any desire. He married many foreign women and worshipped their false gods, violating God's command. Solomon failed to obey the Lord and did evil, so the Lord vowed to tear the kingdom from him, but only after Solomon's death, to honor his father, David.

Solomon concluded that pleasure and everything else was meaningless because death ultimately came to everyone. Solomon's conclusion of man's duty was to fear God and keep his commandments, because God will eventually judge every act of man.

Solomon continued to expand and build the wall of Jerusalem, appointing Jeroboam to be in charge of the workforce. One day, as Jeroboam left Jerusalem, Ahijah the prophet took his own new cloak, tore it into twelve pieces, and told Jeroboam to take ten pieces. Ahijah explained that God had taken the kingdom from Solomon and given it to Jeroboam, who would rule ten tribes, but God would leave Judah and the small tribe of Benjamin to continue David's kingly line. Solomon tried to kill Jeroboam, but Jeroboam fled to Egypt until Solomon died and Solomon's son Rehoboam succeeded him.

The Questions

1. Why do you think Solomon first chose wisdom and then discarded wisdom in favor of something else?
2. When Solomon chose to test what pleasure would provide instead of wisdom, why was he unable to be protected from evil that eventually cost him the kingdom?
3. Why was seeing God twice and receiving from him the most riches and honor inadequate to encourage his obedience?

The Scripture: Eccl 12:13

The Hook Question

Which value or confidence do I hold that would protect me from evil and God's judgment?

OT 25: Israel Divided into Two Kingdoms

The Misconceptions

- Practicing religious duties always results in spiritual power, blessings, and victory for the worshipper.
- Offering religious rituals will satisfy the people that the god will provide peace and safety.
- Political leadership is based upon power and not compassion.

The Passages: 1 Kgs 11:29–31; 12:1–33; 14:7–16, 21–29; 2 Chron 10:1—12:15

The Main Points

1. The northern meeting and rejection of Rehoboam
2. Jeroboam created a false religious system to avoid returning to Jerusalem.
3. Rehoboam established high places for worship in Judah.

The Story

Rehoboam, a son of Solomon, wanted to inherit his father's throne. But, because of Solomon's sins, God had promised to tear the kingdom from Solomon's line after Solomon's death. Jeroboam supervised Solomon's building projects in Jerusalem, but God had promised Jeroboam that he would lead ten of the twelve tribes of the kingdom. Jeroboam feared Solomon and escaped to Egypt until Solomon died. Then Jeroboam returned to Israel at the time Rehoboam went north to claim his kingship of Israel's ten tribes.

The ten tribes of Israel asked Rehoboam for relief from the hard labor and taxes of Solomon's rule. Rehoboam asked Solomon's advisors for advice, and they recommended giving relief. But Rehoboam also asked his friends, and they recommended increasing the labor and taxes, which Rehoboam announced as his decision. The tribes walked away and told Rehoboam to return south to his home in Judah. Rehoboam sent his officer who supervised forced labor to talk to them, but they killed the officer, and Rehoboam fled back to Judah to raise an army. God, however, told them not to attack, and the ten tribes of the north made Jeroboam king.

God previously had required sacrifices to be made at the Jerusalem temple only by the priestly tribe of Levi. Jeroboam realized that northern tribesmen would return south to Jerusalem in Judah to offer sacrifices and enjoy their national feasts and eventually resettle there. To keep the people from returning to Judah, Jeroboam created two golden calves in the northern cities of Dan and Bethel and declared the idols were the gods who had led them out of Egypt. Then Jeroboam appointed priests from any tribe to offer sacrifices and prayers before those idols. Jeroboam also created a new festival one month after the Feast of Tabernacles in Jerusalem. So Jeroboam established his own idols, priests, and feast day, defying God's commands.

God sent a prophet to Bethel to announce his judgment against the false altar and that a man would one day sacrifice the false priests on their high places. Jeroboam, however, never repented of his evil. And Rehoboam continued to build high places to worship false gods in Judah. The Lord sent a prophet to announce judgment against Rehoboam. In Rehoboam's fifth year, Egypt's Pharaoh attacked Jerusalem and greatly weakened Judah.

The Questions

1. Which acts of Jeroboam revealed he either believed or didn't believe in God's promise of rule?
2. What did Rehoboam reveal about his lack of character to make decisions and to rule?
3. How did the people decide if it was right to worship in the north or in Jerusalem?

The Scripture Memory: Ps 40:4

The Hook Questions

What motivated the Israelites to choose to worship in Jerusalem or in the north?

How would I have made the decision where to worship if I had been living in the Northern Kingdom?

OT 26: Prophet Elijah Fought Wicked King Ahab

The Misconceptions

- Familiar spiritual rituals are unquestioned and repeated even if ineffective.
- Courageous spiritual leaders have no spiritual weaknesses.
- Measure God's work by your own firsthand experience.

The Passages: 1 Kgs 16:29—17:1; 18:1—19:18

The Main Points

1. Omri became king of Israel and Judah and made Samaria his capital.
2. Omri's son Ahab and his wife, Jezebel, promoted Baal worship and murdered the Lord's prophets.
3. Prophet Elijah announced a drought and challenged Baal's prophets with sacrifices at Mount Carmel.
4. Elijah fled from Ahab and Jezebel and remained distressed and depressed, but God protected and delivered him.

The Story

The northern ten tribes of Israel and the southern two tribes of Judah and Benjamin often fought each other until Omri, an army captain in Israel, killed both kings and established a new capital in the north called Samaria.

Omri made a treaty with the Sidonian nation by the Mediterranean Sea and sealed it by marrying his son Ahab to a Sidonian princess, Jezebel. The Sidonians worshipped the nature gods Baal and Asherah. Jezebel forced their worship throughout Israel and murdered those prophets God sent to teach the people God's laws.

God's greatest prophet at the time was Elijah. God told Elijah he would stop the rain. The drought lasted three years. Then God told Elijah he would soon end the drought and told Elijah to confront Ahab. Elijah told Ahab to direct the 850 prophets of Baal and Asherah to Mount Carmel to settle which God to worship.

At Mount Carmel, Elijah asked the people, "How long will you change your allegiance between the two opinions? If it is Baal, follow him. But it if is the Lord, follow him." Then Elijah made the challenge, "I am the last of the prophets of the Lord who is left. Let us each take a bull: one sacrificed to Baal and the other to the Lord. We won't set fire to the sacrifice but see which sacrifice is burned by its God."

The Baal prophets went first and worshipped, danced, and called out to Baal. But there was no answer. Then Elijah poured water three times over his sacrifice, and it spilled into a trough around the meat. Suddenly, fire from heaven came down and completely burned up the sacrifice and evaporated the water. The people shouted that the Lord was God, and Elijah commanded them to kill all the 850 prophets of Baal and warned Ahab that a heavy rainstorm was coming.

Ahab and Jezebel tried to kill Elijah—who ran away in fear from them after the contest, still believing he was the last prophet alive. He was anxious and concerned for his life. But the Lord first protected and then fed and encouraged Elijah despite his depression and fears. Then God encouraged Elijah, saying there were still seven thousand believers who had not worshiped or followed Baal, and God gave him a young prophet, Elisha, to mentor until God would take Elijah to heaven in a chariot of fire.

The Questions

1. Why do you think the 850 prophets of the nature gods Baal and Asherah would ignore Elijah's preaching and continue worshipping their gods despite three years of drought?
2. What did Elijah reveal about his character during those drought years and compared to after the challenge on Mount Carmel?
3. What did God reveal about himself while caring for Elijah's fears and depression?

The Scripture Memory: 2 Cor 4:8–9

The Hook Question

Which spiritual practices do I follow that are influenced by my culture or habit that do not bring true fulfillment or spiritual growth to my spirit?

OT 27: God Delayed Assyria's Discipline of Judah

The Misconceptions

- Victory is assured for the strongest and the smartest army.
- The spiritual realm does not affect the physical realm of politics and warfare.

The Passage: 2 Kgs 18–19

The Main Points

1. Israel was disloyal and brought its own punishment through Assyria.
2. Assyria threatened King Hezekiah, who was supported by Isaiah's prophecies.
3. God protected Jerusalem and judged Assyria.

The Story

In the eighth century BC, Assyria was the dominant empire. Ahaz, the king of Judah, ruled from Jerusalem. He declared allegiance to Assyria and paid a large financial tribute to them annually. God's prophet Jeremiah warned Ahaz to remain politically and financially independent, but Ahaz ignored Jeremiah's advice. The Judeans also ignored Jeremiah, violated God's laws, and worshipped the idols and gods of the people they had conquered.

Hoshea, the king of Israel, ruled from Samaria. Hoshea also feared Assyria and paid a large financial tribute annually. God often warned Hoshea through many prophets to repent from worshipping other idols, sacrificing children, and violating God's laws, but Hoshea ignored them. When Assyria installed a new king, Hoshea stopped paying Assyria and, instead, secretly paid Egypt's king for protection. When the king of Assyria discovered Hoshea's relationship to Egypt, he invaded all the land of Israel and began a siege of Samaria that lasted three years until he captured the city and Hoshea. The Assyrian king imprisoned Hoshea in Assyria and deported the Israelites out of the land over the next sixty-five years, as Isaiah had prophesied would happen. The Assyrian king brought other conquered nations into Samaria, leaving only Judah in the land God had promised.

Ahaz died seven years after Samaria fell and the Israelites began their exile. Ahaz's son Hezekiah became king. Unlike his father, Hezekiah committed himself to honoring God. After Assyria's defeat of Samaria, Judah became Assyria's next target. Assyria's commander led his army of over 185,000 to Jerusalem's walls and threatened all the defenders and King Hezekiah of Judah to surrender or be killed as Assyria had done to Samaria and other nations. Hezekiah was terrified by the threats, but he had trusted in the Lord and obeyed the commands of the Lord's covenant. The Lord had been with him as king and had given him success, so Hezekiah prayed humbly and mightily to the Lord for deliverance.

The Lord sent the prophet Isaiah to tell Hezekiah not to fear, because the Assyrians would be cut down and a remnant from Judah would remain in the land. The Lord promised fifteen more years of life to Hezekiah and promised to defend them from the Assyrians. That night, the angel of the Lord killed 185,000 Assyrian soldiers in their camp, and the surviving Assyrians and their king returned the next day to their capital of Nineveh, where the king was murdered by his sons. Hezekiah reigned well during his promised additional years from God and was never troubled again by the Assyrians, who grew weaker.

The Questions

- Which reasons are often used to explain an outbreak of war instead of the result of God's discipline?
- Why could the king trust Isaiah's prophecies of victory over the threat with no preparation for battle?
- Which promises of God were affected by the exile and the kingdom of David? How do we work through believing in God's faithfulness in hope when we see his promises potentially unfulfilled?

The Scripture Memory: Isa 26:4

The Hook Question

Which promises do I believe God will ultimately fulfill whether I am weak or strong, wise or unskilled?

OT 28: The Judeans Were Exiled to Babylon

The Misconceptions

- Politics and military power determine world events.
- Religious practices and faithfulness do not influence world events.
- God does not consider personal or national obedience when determining peace or war.
- God can influence the present but not determine the future.

The Passages: Isa 9; Jer 25:11; 29:5, 10; Ezek 4; 5:5–14; 8; 10; 37:11–14; 40; Dan 7:13–14; 9:2

The Main Points

- The ministry of Isaiah at the time of Assyria
- The ministry of Jeremiah at the time of Babylon
- The ministry of Ezekiel
- The ministry of Daniel

The Story

Judah was spared the defeat and exile that Israel had received from Assyria because Judah's King Hezekiah showed humility and had begun spiritual reforms encouraged by the prophet Isaiah. Isaiah warned Judah not to worship other gods as Israel had done or they would suffer the same punishment as Israel. Isaiah prophesied future devastation from war but also the hope the exiles would return in the future.

After Hezekiah died, his wicked son ruled and led Judah to worship foreign idols. But the son soon died and left his young son Josiah as king. Josiah, however, was raised by godly counselors and Josiah worshiped the Lord like his grandfather. He ordered the temple to be cleansed and the Passover feast to be held again.

While cleaning the temple, priests discovered the law of Moses. Josiah required the priests to read all of the Scriptures to the people. Though the people were unresponsive, Josiah tore his robes in repentance and prayed when he read the judgments God would bring if his covenant and laws were rejected. His fears were confirmed by God through a prophetess. But God promised his judgments would come after Josiah's death.

God sent another prophet, Jeremiah, to Jerusalem, announcing future judgment was certain. They would suffer famine, plague, and war. Then they would be removed from their land and deported to Babylon, now the dominant empire. Jeremiah prophesied their exile would last seventy years, and they should not resist God's discipline, but they should make new and fruitful lives in Babylon. Then God promised he would make a new covenant to replace the old covenant they had broken—a covenant written on their hearts instead of on stone tablets.

Josiah was killed in a battle with Egypt. His son and the people rejected and imprisoned Jeremiah. Instead, they chose to trust false prophets who counseled to resist Babylon and trust in Egypt. Twelve years after Josiah died, King Nebuchadnezzar of Babylon destroyed all the Judean cities and then surrounded and captured Jerusalem, taking the wealth of the temple and deporting the royal family and Judeans to Babylon.

The Questions

1. What do you think motivated the people and the kings to worship false gods instead of the Lord? What benefits do you think they hoped to gain by worshipping foreign gods?
2. Were war and peace determined by the power and military of kings or determined by God in response to the spiritual loyalty or disloyalty of the people?
3. Do the teachings of the prophets about future events—seventy years or longer—encourage acceptance of God's power and plans over the future, or are they merely words to influence their present condition?
4. What did God say that would bring hope to the Israelites?

The Scripture Memory: Jer 29:12

The Hook Question

In what ways does God give me hope even though God and I are both saddened by my sin?

OT 29: Kings Allowed Judah's Return to Rebuild

The Misconceptions

- God leaves those who have been disciplined to recover without his help.
- God permits nations and empires to control their own plans and sovereignty apart from him.
- God no longer cares about the land, because his Spirit left the temple and he removed the people.

The Passages: Jer 25:11; 29:5, 10; Isa 44:28; 45: Ezra 4–10; Neh 6:1–16

The Main Points

1. The return from exile under Cyrus
2. The rebuilding of the temple and altar until stopped by Samaritan opposition
3. Authority granted to continue rebuilding the temple
4. The rebuilding of Jerusalem's walls

The Story

God's plan was to discipline Judah by removing them from their land to Babylon. He never planned to leave them there. His plan included returning them to their promised homeland. The prophet Isaiah prophesied that a man named Cyrus would defeat Babylon and allow them to return. The Persian king Cyrus defeated Babylon in one night and, within a year, issued a command for the exiles to return, rebuild Jerusalem, and lay the foundation for the temple of Jerusalem. Cyrus even returned all the gold and silver that had been taken from the temple to Babylon.

But most of Judah's population were now comfortable in Babylon and didn't want to rebuild the ruins of Jerusalem. However, Levitical priests and the grandson of Judah's last king returned, rebuilt, and consecrated a new altar to offer sacrifices once again.

Cyrus died nine years later and was followed by four Persian kings. Samaritan leaders, enemies of the Jews, wrote the fourth king, asking him to stop the rebuilding of the temple and wall of Jerusalem, warning that the city had a history of rebelling against occupying empires. The king researched history, agreed with the Samaritans, and stopped any rebuilding for the rest of his reign.

But when the fifth Persian king came to power, God sent two prophets to encourage the people to restart rebuilding. The Persian governor asked the Jewish elders, who gave authority for them to rebuild the temple. The elders told their history of God's anger with them and their deportation and then requested the king again to search for King Cyrus's decree to authorize rebuilding the temple. The king found Cyrus's decree and ordered the governor not to stop the rebuilding. The temple was finally completed four years later.

The next Persian king authorized the priest Ezra to return to Jerusalem with more exiles to teach God's laws and oversee the temple sacrifices. Then Nehemiah, the cupbearer to the Persian king, received the king's permission to recruit more exiles to finish rebuilding the Jerusalem wall. Through many decades and slow commitment to return and rebuild, the people finally returned to the land God had promised again and again.

The Questions

1. Why, despite witnessing God's sovereign control and discipline over the kings, nations, and empires, did the exiles fail to recognize the relationship between God's commands and their obedience?
2. Why did the homeland seem significant and important to God but not to the people?
3. What did the rebuilding of the temple and the return of the people reveal about God's future plans?
4. Which prophesied events of the activities of future kings seem most remarkable to you?

The Scripture Memory: Neh 6:15

The Hook Questions

Which current events cause me to wonder if God is in control of my personal life and the governments of the world?

What gives me hope that God is able to bring my personal life and these troubling world events together?

OT 30: God Promised Future Goodness to Israel

The Misconceptions

- God's story was completed when the people returned to their homeland from their exile.
- God no longer cares about Jerusalem and the land; he has left them both to rule themselves like other nations.

The Passages: Zech 8:3–5, 14–15

The Main Points

1. The altar and temple foundation
2. The personal work on houses and farming
3. God's anger spoken through prophets
4. The future plans after the exiles' return

The Story

King Cyrus wrote a decree for Israel to rebuild the altar so Israel could offer morning and evening sacrifices. Israel was to rebuild both the temple and the city. The first year of their return, they rebuilt the altar. The second year, they built the foundation of the temple. But then the Israelites turned from that work to build their own homes and began cultivating the land to return to farming.

God was displeased that they stopped their work building the temple and left Jerusalem unprotected, because there were no walls for the city. And the leaders from neighboring provinces wrote to the new king of the Medes to order the work on the temple to stop, which the king did. Also, the provinces attacked the workers. The result was that all work on the temple and the city stopped for many years, which angered God.

God communicated his anger through prophets who spoke for God, challenging them to regret what they were doing and return to rebuilding the temple and the walls, which is what they did. They even asked Darius, the new king of the Medes, to search his records for Cyrus's decree. Darius found Cyrus's decree in the royal records and immediately allowed the work to continue.

The prophets also spoke about God's plans for the future. Zechariah returned to Jerusalem as a priest, but God called him to speak as his prophet. He said the Lord would return to the land and dwell in Jerusalem. Then Jerusalem would be called the City of Truth, and older men and women would sit in the streets filled with boys and girls playing. God said, "Just as I had determined to bring disaster upon you and showed no pity when your fathers angered me, so now I have determined to do good again to Jerusalem and Judah. Do not be afraid."

The Questions

1. Why was it tempting for the exiles to choose their personal priorities over God's priorities?
2. Which purposes do you believe God had for the land and Jerusalem, for which he was angry they were not getting them done?
3. Why do you think the people felt so discouraged that they would stop working? Why did the exiles feel God's story for them was concluded when they returned to their land?

The Scripture Memory: Zech 7:8–10

The Hook Questions

Is there anything I believe God wants me to do that I haven't treated as a priority?

Why isn't it that important to me?

Chapter 3

Thirty Story Lessons from the Life of Jesus

J 1: Announcement of Jesus's Birth

The Misconceptions

- Jesus's birth announcement was unknown at the time but created only after Jesus became famous.
- God cannot appear in flesh but only in spirit.
- Jesus was a prophet and was not identified as a Savior, Son of God, or Eternal King until after his death.

The Passages: Luke 1:26–38; 2:1–18, 22–38

The Main Points

1. Gabriel announced to Mary she would have a supernatural birth of a future king.
2. The birth was announced by shepherds in Bethlehem.
3. Jesus was identified and his role announced to all by two old saints in the temple.
4. Foreign kings from the east arrived to worship, causing Herod to attempt to kill Jesus.

The Story

God sent the angel Gabriel to announce a coming miracle to Mary, a young virgin pledged to marry Joseph. Gabriel told her she would become pregnant with a son who would be called the Son of the Most High and given the throne of his ancestor, King David. He would be named Jesus, and his kingdom would never end. Mary asked, "How can this be, because I've never been with a man?" Gabriel answered the Holy Spirit would miraculously cause her to become pregnant without a human father. Then an angel assured Joseph that Mary had not been unfaithful to him, but God had miraculously created the baby.

The night of Jesus's birth, Joseph and Mary were in Bethlehem—the historic hometown of King David. Shepherds out in their fields watching their flocks that night saw an angel who announced the birth of a Savior for all the people. And then the sky was filled with angels, all praising God. Just as suddenly, the angels disappeared, and the shepherds went into

Bethlehem to find the baby. Then they publicly announced what the angels had told them to everyone.

After Mary recovered, she and her husband went to Jerusalem to consecrate and offer a sacrifice at the temple for their son, Jesus. When they entered the temple, they were met by an old and righteous man who held Jesus in his arms and, by the Spirit of God, identified Jesus as the one who was the salvation and the glory of Israel and the light to gentiles. Then an old woman who worshipped constantly in the temple spoke about Jesus to those looking for the redemption of Jerusalem.

After returning to Bethlehem, they were visited by magi, influential leaders in rituals and customs in another country, who studied the stars and had seen in them a sign of a king's birth. They had first met with King Herod and asked him and his priests where the baby who was born to be king lived. The Hebrew priests referred to a prophecy that the Messiah would be born in Bethlehem. So the magi went to Bethlehem and left rich treasure with Mary and Joseph for Jesus. Joseph was warned by the Holy Spirit to depart, so they left for Egypt. Shortly afterward, King Herod ordered the deaths of any boys born within the previous two years, to kill this baby king. The family remained in Egypt until the death of King Herod before returning to Israel.

The Questions

1. Which people in the story gave a personal confirmation that the birthnight was exceptional and miraculous and known to all of Bethlehem and to the magi? How could these reports of a miraculous night be disproved?
2. Why do you think God wanted to make the birthnight known to all?
3. What does Herod's killing of all the infants reveal about his belief of the prophecy?

The Scripture Memory: Luke 2:10–11

The Hook Questions

How would I have first reacted if I had been a shepherd in the field that night?

Would I have stayed in the field, gone someplace to tell others, or gone to the birthplace to get more information?

J 2: Jesus Changed Water to Wine

The Misconceptions
- Jesus revealed his powers only to those who believed in him.
- Jesus was powerless to overrule natural laws.

The Passage: John 2:1–11

The Main Points
1. The wedding celebration ran out of wine.
2. Jesus changed gallons of water into the finest wine.
3. Jesus revealed his glory, and then the disciples put their faith in him.

The Story

Jesus was invited to a wedding in Cana in the region of Galilee. He brought his followers, or disciples, with him. His mother also attended the wedding and likely helped to serve in the celebration. Later, she came to Jesus and told him of a problem; they were running out of wine. She expected Jesus to fix the problem, but Jesus answered that it wasn't the right time to call attention to his ministry. Mary turned to the servants and told them to do whatever Jesus asked them to do.

Jesus told the servants to fill six nearby jars with water, each holding twenty-five to thirty gallons. Then Jesus told them to draw the water out to present to the master of the banquet. The master was amazed when he tasted it, because it was excellent wine. Only the servants knew the wine had come from water. But the banquet master went to the groom and complimented him that most people brought out the best wine at the beginning of the party and the cheapest at the end, but he had brought out the best wine now. This was the first miracle Jesus did in Galilee to reveal his glory, causing his disciples to put their faith in him.

Thirty Story Lessons from the Life of Jesus

The Questions

1. What did the disciples see that convinced them that Jesus had performed a miracle?
2. Why do you think each of the disciples decided to follow Jesus to the wedding if they didn't already have faith in him?
3. After at first declining his mother's request because of his ministry strategy, why do you think Jesus changed his mind about solving the wine problem?

The Scripture Memory: John 2:11

The Hook Question

If I had only heard, but not seen, a miracle from other reports, what would be important for me to know before agreeing a miracle had happened?

J 3: Jesus Recruited His Disciples

The Misconceptions

- Past experiences determine future ministry.
- Obedience to Jesus's commands requires first having faith.
- Being a sinner disqualifies a person from being called to ministry.

The Passage: Luke 5:1–11

The Main Points

1. Jesus taught at the seashore near Simon Peter's boat.
2. Jesus told Peter to go to deep water for a catch.
3. Peter obeyed Jesus and got an overwhelming catch.
4. Peter confessed he was a sinner, and Jesus recruited him instead.

The Story

While Jesus was teaching at the seashore, he noticed two fishing boats pulled ashore for the fishermen to wash their nets. Jesus got in one of the boats. It belonged to Simon Peter, and Jesus asked to be pushed out a small ways into the sea so he could speak to the growing crowd of listeners.

When Jesus finished, he asked Simon Peter to put the boat out to deeper water and let down the nets for a catch. Simon Peter said, "We worked all night and didn't catch anything, but because you say so, we'll let down the nets." When the fishermen pulled the nets back up, they were filled with so many fish that the nets started to tear, and they called to their partners from the other boat for help. When their partners arrived, both boats were so filled with fish they began to sink!

When Simon Peter witnessed this, he fell to his knees before Jesus and said, "Go from me, Lord, for I am a sinful man!" Jesus replied, "Don't be afraid. From now on you will catch men." After the men pulled the fish on shore, three of those fishermen—James, John, and Peter—left everything to follow Jesus.

Thirty Story Lessons from the Life of Jesus

The Questions

1. Why did Peter, an experienced professional fisherman, obey Jesus though he had spent the night fishing without success?
2. What motivated Peter to tell Jesus to go from him as he was a sinner? Was he relying on faith?
3. How would the story have ended if Peter had made the decision to rely on his experience and not obey Jesus to go to the deeper waters?

The Scripture Memory: Luke 5:5

The Hook Question

What would encourage me to obey Jesus's commands even if I had little or no faith in him as a miracle worker?

J 4: Jesus Fed Five Thousand Who Heard Him

The Misconceptions

- Jesus was not actively involved in common activities or needs.
- We are limited by the supplies and preparations we bring to a needed activity.
- Miracles are always very public, to gain notice.

The Passages: Matt 14:15–21; Mark 6:35–44; Luke 9:12–17; John 6:4–13

The Main Points

1. Jesus taught five thousand people all day into dinnertime.
2. Jesus gave directions to the disciples to prepare meals for all.
3. Jesus fed five thousand with a young boy's five loaves and two fish, with twelve baskets left over.
4. The people responded by trying to force Jesus to be king, but Jesus escaped.

The Story

Jesus was teaching and healing near the Sea of Galilee. As evening came, there were five thousand men and their families still present. The disciples told Jesus he should stop to allow the people to find food for dinner, but Jesus replied they should not stop and told the disciples, "You feed them."

The disciples had no food but found a young boy with five loaves and two fishes and reported that to Jesus. They reported to Jesus all the food available, and they had no money to buy enough food, but Jesus told them, "Bring the food to me." Then Jesus directed all the people to sit in smaller circles of fifty or one hundred people.

Jesus looked up and thanked God for the food before breaking the bread and dividing the two fish into baskets and then gave the food to the disciples to distribute. When everyone had eaten all they needed, they collected the leftover broken bread and fish and put it all into twelve baskets!

Many people reacted by wanting to force Jesus to become their king. When Jesus recognized this reaction, he told his disciples to immediately get in a boat and row to another city. Jesus, however, withdrew to a mountain where he prayed by himself.

The Questions

1. Why do you think Jesus didn't take the initiative to address dinner needs but waited for the disciples to raise the question?
2. Which faith or obedience was required of the people for this great miracle to happen?
3. How could the miracle be denied when witnessed by five thousand witnesses who were there, handled and ate the food, and put the leftovers in the baskets in the miracle?
4. Why didn't Jesus take the opportunity to agree to the people's wishes that he be their king?

The Scripture Memory: Matt 7:7

The Hook Questions

Is it more important for me to know that a miracle happened, how it happened, or why it happened?

Which answer would influence me to describe the miracle to others?

J 5: Jesus Walked on Water

The Misconceptions

- Jesus cannot change physical matter or laws.
- Jesus is unaware of everyone's situation and the needs of those who are beyond his presence.
- Jesus cannot give full attention to everyone's needs or situations at once.

The Passages: Matt 14:24–33; Mark 6:47–52; John 6:16–21

The Main Points

1. Jesus sent the disciples to another city by boat without him.
2. A storm raged at sea, but Jesus walked on the water to the boat.
3. Peter walked a few steps on water, then lost faith and began to sink until rescued.
4. The wind died down after Peter and Jesus got into the boat.

The Story

After feeding the five thousand men and their families, the people wanted to force Jesus to become their king. Jesus reacted to the situation by directing his disciples to get in the boat and go to another city on the lake while he went up a mountain alone to pray. As the disciples rowed about four miles into the middle of the sea late in the night, a terrible storm came, battering their boat so badly they feared for their lives. But Jesus was away.

Then the disciples saw someone walking on the water toward them. Thinking it was a ghost, they became even more terrified. But it was Jesus walking up to the boat, and he called out, "Take courage. It is I. Do not be afraid." One of the disciples, Peter, said, "Lord, if it really is you, command me to come to you on the water." Jesus said, "Come!" So Peter got out of the boat and walked to Jesus. But when Peter looked at the wind and the waves, he became afraid and began to sink. He cried out, "Lord save me!" Jesus caught him and said, "You have so little faith! Why did you doubt?" When they both got in the boat, the wind immediately stopped and all the disciples were amazed, because they still had not fully realized all that Jesus's feeding of the five thousand had revealed about his true identity.

The Questions

1. How do you think the disciples thought about Jesus after both the feeding of five thousand from little food and Peter and Jesus walking on the water?
2. Which types of growth in the faith of the disciples did Jesus hope to find exposed by the dangers of the storm?
3. Jesus had commanded the disciples to cross the lake in a boat, so why did they still fear for their lives? What was still missing in their understanding about Jesus?

The Scripture Memory: Ps 89:9

The Hook Question

Why would I not believe that Jesus would be praying for me when I am facing an issue that requires my courage and trust?

J 6: Jesus Stopped a Storm at Sea

The Misconceptions

- What happens to Jesus's followers is beyond Jesus's control.
- Natural dangers are outside Jesus's powers to control.
- Though Jesus has compassion for those struggling, he does not protect them from those struggles.

The Passages: Matt 8:18, 23–27; Mark 4:35–41; Luke 8:22–25

The Main Points

1. Jesus, tired from ministry, told his disciples to go across the Sea of Galilee in a boat.
2. A furious storm frightened the disciples while Jesus slept in the boat.
3. The fearful disciples woke Jesus, who stopped the storm and challenged their small faith.

The Story

Jesus had been surrounded by large crowds and was getting very tired from ministering. So Jesus told his disciples to get a boat and cross over to the other side of the Sea of Galilee. Jesus quickly fell asleep in the back of the boat.

However, a furious storm developed over the sea, the wind stirred up the waves, and the boat was almost swamped. But the storm did not awaken Jesus, so the disciples woke him up and said, "Teacher, don't you care if we drown?"

Jesus got up, rebuked the waves, and commanded them, "Quiet! Be still!" The wind died down, and the sea became completely calm. Then Jesus asked the disciples, "Why are you so afraid? Do you still not have faith?" And the disciples were amazed and said, "What kind of man is this, that even the winds and the sea obey him?"

The Questions

1. Which beliefs of faith should the disciples have been applying?
2. What were the priority concerns the disciples had? Could those concerns have been present without the storm's presence?
3. Do you think the disciples grew more in applying faith to their concerns, or did they just grow in their amazement?

The Scripture Memory: Matt 8:27

The Hook Question

Which current concern could I ask Jesus to resolve, to grow my faith in him?

J 7: Jesus Healed from a Distance

The Misconceptions
- Jesus's healings were psychologically influenced.
- Jesus's healings were adjustments made naturally by physical manipulations.
- Jesus's healings were spiritual battles with demons.
- Jesus's healings were performed as magic.
- Healing is granted to those who are worthy.
- Believing is based upon personally seeing a miracle.

The Passages: John 4:46-54; Matt 8:5-13; Luke 7:1-10

The Main Points
- The official in Cana begged Jesus to heal his son in Capernaum.
- Jesus said the son would live.
- The centurion in Capernaum asked Jesus to command his servant be healed from paralysis without going to the centurion's home.
- Jesus replied the servant would be healed as the centurion believed.

The Story

Jesus had entered the town of Cana when he was quickly stopped by an official who begged Jesus to go to the town of Capernaum to heal his dying son. Jesus replied, "You people won't believe unless you see miracles." The official begged again, and Jesus said, "Go home, for your son is healed." As he returned to Capernaum, his servants met him on the road and told him his son lived. He asked when his son had gotten better, and they answered, "Around one p.m.," which was when Jesus had told him his son would live. Then he and his household believed in Jesus.

After several days, Jesus went to Capernaum, and he was met by a Roman centurion who asked Jesus to heal one of his servants who was paralyzed and suffering terribly. Jesus told him he would go and heal him, but the centurion said, "Don't trouble yourself for I'm unworthy of your coming to my house. But, I give orders that are obeyed by others. You only need to say the word, and my servant will be healed." Jesus said to the crowd, "I haven't found such great faith like this anywhere in Israel." And he told the centurion, "Go. It will be done just as you believed it would." And the centurion immediately returned home and found the servant healed.

The Questions

1. How would you compare Jesus's responses to the requests from the official and from the centurion? What did Jesus observe that caused him to evaluate their faiths differently?

2. Why do physicians usually require meeting face-to-face with sick people before they attempt healing? Why didn't Jesus need to meet face-to-face with these seriously ill people?

3. How did Jesus heal? What did he do? What does that reveal about his power?

4. The confirmation of each healing was by witnesses who were not physically near Jesus. Why was that significant, and how could their testimony support the truth of Jesus's healing?

The Scripture Memory: Matt 8:13

The Hook Question

Do I depend on personally seeing a miracle before believing, or can I learn and believe the report of others who experienced the presence of Jesus?

J 8: Jesus Healed a Man Born Blind

The Misconceptions

- Disabilities are God's judgments for the sins of either the disabled or their parents.
- Peoples' physical condition reflects their spiritual condition.
- Miracles cannot prove divine authority unless they also fit in man's theological categories.
- Those who report a personal witness of Jesus are not persecuted.

The Passage: John 9:1–38

The Main Points

1. The disciples asked if the sins of the blind man or of his father caused the man to be born blind.
2. Jesus put mud on the man's eyes and told him to wash his eyes in the pool, and then he could see.
3. The Pharisees questioned the blind man and his parents, rejecting the healing of Jesus and removing the man from the synagogue because the healing took place on the Sabbath.
4. Jesus searched for the man and identified himself to him, and the man worshipped him.

The Story

As Jesus walked with his disciples, they met a man blind since birth. The disciples asked Jesus, "Who sinned, this man or his father, that he would be born blind?" And Jesus answered, "Neither. He was born blind to reveal a work of God through his life." Jesus spit in the dirt to make mud, which he put on the man's eyes and directed him to wash off in the pool of Siloam. After the man cleaned his eyes in the pool of Siloam, he could see!

Others first thought the man must be someone who looked like the blind man, but he said, "No! It is me! I can see now," and then described how Jesus healed him. Some Pharisees argued it couldn't have happened, because it was on the Sabbath, when healings couldn't happen. So they asked him who he believed Jesus was, and he answered, "He is a prophet."

The Pharisees called his parents to confirm he was their son and was born blind. They called the man back to describe again how he was healed. They accused Jesus of being a sinner. Furthermore, they didn't know from where Jesus had arrived. The man found their lack of knowledge about Jesus to be remarkable and said, "Whether he is a sinner or not, I don't know. One thing I do know is that once I was blind, but now I see. We know that God doesn't listen to sinners but to the obedient, godly man. Nobody has ever opened the eyes of a man born blind before. If this man were not from God, he could not do anything."

His answer so angered the Pharisees, they threw him out of the synagogue. When Jesus heard what they had done to the man, Jesus found him and asked, "Do you believe in the Son of Man?" The man asked, "Who is he?" Jesus answered, "The one speaking with you now." And the man replied, "Lord, I believe," and he worshipped Jesus.

The Questions

1. The religious leaders asked the man his perspective based on their theological beliefs, but the man answered the question nontheologically, which led to which judgment?
2. Did the mud have medicinal value? What role did the mud play in the miracle?
3. Why is it wrong to give Jesus only two options by which to interpret a situation?
4. What do you learn about the Pharisees from their rejection of the miracle?

The Scripture Memory: John 9:25

The Hook Questions

Have I ever prayed for God to work in my situation while also limiting God's response to how I wanted God to respond or what the results were to be?

Why would placing those limits defeat my requests?

J 9: Jesus Raised the Widow's Son from the Dead

The Misconceptions

- God is unaffected by our personal tragedies or crises.
- Everyone is responsible to satisfy their own personal needs.

The Passage: Luke 7:11–23

The Main Points

1. Jesus and his followers met mourners carrying the only son of a widow, to bury him.
2. Jesus comforted the widow and then raised her son from the dead.
3. The crowds marveled and praised God as news of the miracle traveled broadly.

The Story

Jesus, his disciples, and many followers approached the town of Nain when they came upon a large crowd of people carrying the body of a dead young man out of the town to be buried. He was the only son of his widowed mother. Jesus's heart went out to the woman, and he went to comfort her and told her not to cry. He then went to the men carrying the coffin and touched the coffin, so they stopped and put it down. Jesus commanded the dead man in the coffin and said, "Young man, get up!" And the man sat up and began to talk. Then Jesus took him and gave him back to his mother.

The crowds of people were in awe and began praising God and saying, "A great prophet has appeared to us" and "God has come to help his people." And this news of what Jesus did was spread throughout Judea and the countryside.

The Questions

1. What caused Jesus to raise the young man from the dead even though he hadn't been asked? What does that reveal about Jesus's requirement to have a measure of mature faith for him to respond miraculously?
2. Why is the detail that the young man was the only son of a widow important? Which concerns would the mother have had about her future?
3. Why would this miracle be so difficult to deny?

The Scripture Memory: Matt 6:7–8

The Hook Question

If I had been in one of the crowds and told a friend about seeing this miracle and they didn't believe me, would I be insulted, frustrated, concerned about what my friend was missing, or simply move on and ignore their opinion?

J 10: Jesus Raised Jairus's Daughter from the Dead

The Misconceptions

- Death is more powerful than Jesus's ability to heal.
- Jesus's influence and power was limited to teaching and healing.

The Passages: Matt 9:18–26; Mark 5:21–43; Luke 8:40–56

The Main Points

1. Jairus asked Jesus to heal his dying daughter.
2. After a woman was healed, Jairus was told his daughter had died and not to bother Jesus.
3. Jesus told Jairus not to be afraid but believe and told the mourners she was just asleep.
4. Jesus brought the spirit back to the girl, and she was resurrected.

The Story

Jesus and the disciples entered a village and were soon surrounded by a crowd. The leader of the local synagogue, Jairus, came to Jesus and said, "My twelve-year-old daughter is dying. Please come and put your hands on her so she will be healed and live." As Jesus began to leave with Jairus, another woman touched Jesus and was immediately healed of her bleeding. While Jesus talked with her, members of Jairus's household told Jairus, "Your daughter died. Why bother the teacher any longer?"

Jesus ignored their report and told Jairus, "Do not be afraid but believe." Jesus took three of his disciples—James, Peter, and John—and they went to Jairus's home. When they arrived, the mourners were in the home. Jesus asked why they were mourning and said, "She is not dead but asleep!" The mourners laughed at Jesus and ridiculed him. Jesus sent them out of the house, so only the father, mother, the three disciples, and Jesus remained.

Jesus took her hand and said, "Little girl, get up!" And the spirit returned to the girl, and she stood up and walked around. Jesus told the parents to get some food for the girl and asked them not to spread the story of what had happened.

The Questions

1. Which opinion about Jesus was revealed by the household of Jairus saying, "Don't bother the teacher anymore"?
2. After overhearing the news of the death given to Jairus, which command did Jesus give instead of words of consolation? What might Jairus have expected Jesus to say?
3. Which emotions do you think Jairus felt when he arrived at home after Jesus's command to ignore fear and simply believe?
4. Which opinion about Jesus did the mourners reveal about Jesus and their own compassion? How did Jesus respond to them?

The Scripture Memory: Mark 5:36

The Hook Question

Which discouragements, fears, or concerns do I have now that I think Jesus may tell me to ignore and believe in him instead?

J 11: Jesus Raised Lazarus from the Dead

The Misconceptions

- Jesus was only a prophet who could heal those who were ill.
- Resurrection is a one-time event for all people at the end of the age.
- Jesus's response was influenced by his emotions.

The Passage: John 11:1–46

The Main Points

1. Jesus was told of Lazarus's illness, waited two days until Lazarus died, and then left.
2. Jesus talked with Martha and Mary, who said Lazarus wouldn't have died if Jesus had arrived earlier.
3. Jesus raised Lazarus; some rejoiced, but the Pharisees and Sanhedrin plotted Jesus's death.

The Story

Two sisters, Mary and Martha, lived with their brother Lazarus near Jerusalem. They were deeply loved by Jesus, so when Lazarus was very ill, they sent a message to inform Jesus. Jesus, however, told his disciples, "This will not end in death but will glorify God, so that his Son will be glorified through it." He waited two more days and then said, "Lazarus has died. For your sakes, I'm glad I wasn't there, so you will believe. Let's go to him."

When Jesus and the disciples arrived, Martha greeted him, saying, "If you had been here, he wouldn't have died. But I know God will give you whatever you ask." Jesus answered, "Your brother will rise again." Martha replied, "I know he will rise again on the last day." But Jesus answered her, saying, "I am the resurrection and the life. Anyone who believes in me will live and never die. Do you believe that?" Martha answered, "Yes, Lord. I believe you are the Anointed One and the Son of God." Then she left to tell Mary that Jesus was outside and had asked for her.

When Mary saw Jesus, she was crying and said, "If you had been here, my brother would not have died." All the mourners following Mary also said, "He healed the blind man, so he could have kept Lazarus from dying." Jesus was also deeply moved and crying.

Jesus asked where they had put Lazarus. It was in a cave with a stone rolled across it. Jesus told them to take away the stone, but Mary said, "He's been dead for four days, so the smell will be terrible." But they moved the stone. Jesus first prayed to God for the benefit of the crowd to recognize God was honoring Jesus's prayer. Then Jesus commanded, "Lazarus, come out!" And Lazarus came out, still wrapped in gravecloths, which Jesus told those nearby to remove.

Many who saw this put their faith in Jesus. Others went to the Pharisees and told them what had happened. The Pharisees and the chief priests plotted how to kill Jesus.

The Questions

1. What do you think Martha, Mary, and the mourners expected from Jesus?
2. Why do you think Jesus waited the two days until Lazarus died before he went to them?
3. What was the ultimate purpose for this resurrection that was greater than Jesus coming earlier and healing Lazarus?
4. Why did the Pharisees and chief priests try to kill Jesus?

The Scripture Memory: John 11:25

The Hook Question

Which emotions do I think Jesus may have about me when I die?

J 12: Jesus Taught to Love Enemies

The Misconceptions

- Treat your enemies with the same hostility they treat you or others.
- You must love, greet, or do good things only to those who love you.
- Hate your enemies.
- Do not lend money to those who will not repay you.

The Passages: Matt 5:38–48; Luke 6:27–36

The Main Points

1. Jesus taught that cultural responses of repaying evil with evil, loving your friends but hating your enemy, and lending only to those who can repay do not reflect God's responses.
2. We are rewarded with grace when responding as our heavenly Father, who responds to the ungrateful with mercy and sends rain upon both the righteous and unrighteous.

The Story

Crowds came from near and far away to hear Jesus teach and also to be healed. One time, Jesus went to the side of a mountain so all the crowd could hear him teach.

Jesus said, "You've heard it said, 'An eye for an eye and a tooth for a tooth,' but I say you shouldn't resist an evil person." Jesus also said, "You've heard it said, 'Love your neighbor and hate your enemy,' but I say you should love your enemies and pray for those who mistreat and persecute you." Then he said, "All people love those who love them, and lend money to those they know will pay them back. Those responses don't bring grace or favor. Instead, I say, love your enemies, do good, and lend without expecting to be repaid. Then you will receive grace and favor, your reward will be great, and you will be sons of God because your heavenly Father is kind to the ungrateful and wicked. God causes the sun to rise on both the evil and the good and sends rain on both the righteous and the unrighteous. So do to others as you would have them do to you, and be merciful just as your heavenly Father in heaven is merciful."

Thirty Story Lessons from the Life of Jesus

The Questions

1. Why would personal revenge or compensation not be encouraged by Jesus?
2. What is the benefit of responding in grace and mercy to those who have wronged you?
3. Have you ever insulted or been angry with God? How did he respond to you?

The Scripture Memory: Luke 6:35

The Hook Question

Whom do I think about when I hope the Lord won't ask me to be merciful and loving to them in the future? Why?

J 13: Jesus Taught to Love Strangers

The Misconceptions

- Maintaining personal ritual cleanliness is more important than serving others.
- Neighbors share equal social status with another.
- Neighbors share a common cultural identity.

The Passage: Luke 10:25–37

The Main Points

1. A teacher of the law asked Jesus what he must do to inherit eternal life.
2. The teacher tried to justify himself by asking who was his neighbor.
3. Jesus told a story of a priest, a Levite, and a Samaritan and their own expressions of either denying or giving compassion.
4. The teacher identified the Samaritan as the neighbor because of compassion for the victim.

The Story

An expert of Jewish law asked Jesus what he had to do to inherit eternal life. Jesus asked him what the law said, and the expert answered, "Love the Lord your God with all your heart, soul, mind, and strength and love your neighbor as yourself." Jesus replied that he had answered correctly, but the expert—knowing he couldn't meet that standard—turned away, asking, "But who is my neighbor?" Jesus answered his excuse by telling this story:

A man was traveling on the road and was beaten by robbers who left him for dead. A priest came by and, when he saw the man, crossed to the other side of the road and continued on. So did another Levite priest. But then came a Samaritan—from a people despised by the Jews—who pitied the victim, bandaged his wounds, and poured oil and wine on them to help healing. Then he put the man on his own donkey and took him to an inn where he cared for him. The next day, he paid the innkeeper two silver coins to continue caring for the victim and promised he would return to reimburse any extra expenses the innkeeper had to pay.

Then Jesus asked the teacher, "Which of these three was the neighbor to the victim?" And the expert answered, "The one who had compassion on him." And Jesus said, "Go and do the same."

The Questions

1. Why would the expert still feel he had to justify himself after correctly quoting the law?
2. How would you identify someone as your neighbor? Is it someone who lives near you? Is everyone living by you a friend? Is it someone who does the same activities as you do? Is it only a close friend?
3. Which definition did Jesus believe identified a neighbor? Why do you think Jesus specifically chose a priest, a Levite, and a Samaritan to be in the story?
4. How did Jesus's story cause the law expert to recognize his own values are those being challenged by Jesus?

The Scripture Memory: Matt 9:13

The Hook Question

How does limiting my love and mercy reveal more about my own character than defining another person as unworthy?

J 14: Jesus Taught Personal Righteousness

The Misconceptions

- Common cultural understanding of religious sayings should be unquestioned.
- It is possible to obey all Jewish law perfectly as taught by religious teachers.
- Our righteous standing before God is determined by the performance of religious duties and perfect obedience of commands.

The Passage: Matt 5:21–44

The Main Points

1. Anger is murder, lustful thoughts are adultery, and divorce should be only for marital infidelity.
2. A yes or no response is sufficient, and sworn oaths should not be used.
3. Do not respond to evil with revenge, but offer blessing instead.

The Story

Large crowds followed Jesus to hear him teach. Jesus would challenge his listeners to reexamine and question religious teachings that were familiar to them but incomplete. These had allowed people to think they were righteous, but their understanding of the law was only partial and didn't challenge their personal spiritual living.

Jesus said to the crowd, "You have heard it said, 'Do not murder, and anyone who murders will be subject to judgment.' But I tell you that anyone who is angry with his brother will be subject to judgment.

"You have heard it said, 'Do not commit adultery.' But I tell you that anyone who looks at a woman lustfully has already committed adultery with her in his heart.

"It has been said, 'Anyone who divorces his wife must give her a certificate of divorce.' But I tell you that anyone who divorces his wife, except for marital unfaithfulness, causes her to commit adultery, and anyone who marries a woman so divorced commits adultery.

"You have heard it said, 'Do not break your oath.' But I tell you, do not swear at all, but let your yes be yes and your no be no. Anything beyond that comes from the evil one.

"You have heard it said, 'An eye for an eye and a tooth for a tooth.' But I say to you, do not resist an evil person. If someone strikes you on the cheek, give the person your other cheek. If someone wants to sue you and take your clothes, give him your coat also."

The Questions

1. Why would Jesus challenge people's thoughts about familiar religious sayings?
2. Would it be possible for anyone to insist on their personal righteousness on the same basis as Jesus used here?
3. The sayings describe actions we do or don't do. Jesus added that personal, spiritual attitudes related to these actions were also capable of being judged. How can we control our personal attitudes?

The Scripture Memory: Matt 7:1–3

The Hook Question

Is it unfair to evaluate my own personal righteousness by my thoughts and motivations instead of only by my actions?

J 15: Jesus Taught against Self-Righteousness

The Misconceptions

- I am righteous, because I don't commit evil deeds like other people.
- I am righteous, because I practice religious duties like prayer, fasting, and tithing.
- I work to gain more righteousness than other people.

The Passage: Luke 18:9–14

The Main Points

1. Jesus told a parable of a Pharisee and a tax collector going to pray at the temple.
2. The Pharisee was confident in his righteousness, because he didn't do evil like others but performed righteous acts.
3. The tax collector confessed he was a sinner and pleaded for mercy.
4. The tax collector, and not the Pharisee, was justified.

The Story

Jesus told a story to challenge those who were confident of their own righteous standing before God. Jesus said, "Two men went to the temple to pray. One man was a Pharisee, and the other was a tax collector. The Pharisee stood up to pray about himself, saying, 'I thank you that I am not like all other men who are robbers, evildoers, or adulterers, or even this tax collector. I fast twice a week and give a tenth of all I get.' The tax collector, however, wouldn't even look up to heaven. He beat his breast and pleaded, 'God have mercy on me, a sinner.'"

Jesus said the tax collector, and not the confident Pharisee, went home justified by God, because everyone who exalts themselves will be humbled, and those who humble themselves will be exalted.

The Questions

1. What was the basis of the Pharisee's appeal before God?
2. What was the basis of the tax collector's appeal before God?
3. What does God listen for in a person's prayer to him?
4. Why would this story threaten a Pharisee?
5. Did you consider your response to be better than the Pharisee's response? Should you be judged for that?

The Scripture Memory: 1 Pet 5:5–6

The Hook Question

Are there any religious duties or practices that I do to earn my righteousness before God?

J 16: Jesus Taught about Greed and Worry

The Misconceptions

- It is justifiable and good financial management to preserve my wealth rather than to give it away.
- It is more important to increase my possessions for the future than to give to God for the present.
- Increasing wealth for my future is good financial planning and never greedy.

The Passages: Luke 12:13–34; Matt 6:19–21, 25–34

The Main Points

1. A man cried out, asking about his demand for an inheritance.
2. Jesus warned about greed and told a parable about a rich man keeping wealth but suddenly dying and his wealth going to another.
3. Rely upon God to supply food and clothing for life, seeing that he even provides for the birds and makes nature beautiful, so do not worry about God's faithful provision.
4. Seek God's kingdom first and give to the poor, and God will supply what you need to live.

The Story

A crowd had surrounded Jesus, when someone yelled, "Tell my brother to divide the inheritance with me!" Jesus asked him, "Who appointed me to be a judge? Watch out! Be on guard against all forms of greed. A man's life does not consist of his possessions!"

Then he told a parable: "One year, a rich man had such a large harvest his barns could not contain it. He decided to tear down his barns and build larger barns to store all the harvest and to eat, drink, and be merry for the remainder of his life. But God said, 'You fool! Tonight I will take your life, and then who will get what you saved for yourself?'" Then Jesus said, "This is what will happen to anyone who stores for himself but is not rich toward God!"

Jesus told his disciples not to worry about their lives and what they wore or ate, because life was more than food or clothes. Birds don't sow or reap food or have barns, but God feeds them. And grass that can be burned the next day is made beautiful by God, who dresses it with flowers. Because you are more valuable than birds or grass, God will provide your food and clothes. Worrying about those things is worthless, because your worries can't add even one hour to your life. Nonbelievers rush after those things, but you are to seek God's kingdom first, and all these things will also be provided by God.

So sell what you have, and give to the poor. Put your treasures in heaven, where they can't be stolen or destroyed by moths. For wherever your treasure is, your heart will be there.

The Questions

1. What do you think the rich man should have done with his great harvest?
2. How can you recognize when someone becomes greedy? Is a generous attitude revealed only by the size of the gift or by the faith and compassion that motivate the giving?
3. Can a poor person be greedy? What would be the connection with faith?
4. Why does Jesus talk about worry as an indicator of living by faith or by greed?

The Scripture Memory: Matt 6:33

The Hook Questions

What do I worry about most often?

How would asking God to increase my faith affect my levels of worry?

J 17: Jesus Taught Samaritan about Worship

The Misconceptions

- Religious cultural traditions establish unquestioned foundational truths.
- True worship of God is formed out of cultural practices rather than religious questions.
- God does not seek after us, but we must seek after God.

The Passage: John 4:4–42

The Main Points

1. Jesus asked for water from a Samaritan woman at a well.
2. Jesus offered the woman water to remove thirst eternally.
3. She viewed Jesus as prophet and relied upon her worship traditions and hope for Messiah.
4. Jesus revealed himself as Messiah, and she told her village, resulting in many believers.

The Story

Jesus was traveling through Samaria and stopped at a well to ask a woman for water. She was amazed by his request, because Jews avoided any contact with Samaritans. But Jesus said if she knew who he was, she would ask him for water, because his water would bring eternal life and satisfy thirst forever. But when she asked for that water, Jesus told her to call her husband. She replied that she had no husband. Jesus agreed with her and said she previously had had five husbands and was now living unmarried with another man.

So the woman concluded that Jesus was a prophet and said, "Our fathers worshipped on this mountain, but you Jews claim we must worship in Jerusalem." Jesus replied that the time was coming when worship would not be in either place: "You Samaritans worship what you don't know; we worship what we do know, because salvation is from the Jews. The time has come when true worshippers will worship in spirit and truth, because God is spirit and those are the worshippers the Father seeks." The woman answered, "I know the Messiah is coming, and when he comes, he will explain everything to us." Jesus answered, "I am he."

The woman ran to tell the villagers about how Jesus told her everything about herself and that he could be the Messiah. The villagers rushed out to meet Jesus and urged him to stay with them for two days. Many believed in Jesus and said to the woman, "We no longer believe because of what you said, because we've now heard him for ourselves and believe he is the Savior of the world!"

The Questions

1. What did Jesus find wrong in the woman's conclusions about worship and for which reason?
2. Why do you think Jesus used water and thirst to represent eternal life?
3. What does this story teach about man seeking God and knowing how to worship him?
4. How did God the Father use Jesus and the woman to seek spiritual worshippers?

The Scripture Memory: Matt 5:6

The Hook Question

If I had encountered Jesus and had a face-to-face conversation with him as the woman had, would I have described the entire conversation to my friends, or would I have kept it private? Why?

J 18: Jesus Taught about Father and Sons

The Misconceptions

- Honor and rewards must be earned by faithfulness.
- Restoration can be earned back by the dishonored.
- A motivation for obedience is earning a reward.

The Passage: Luke 15:11–32

The Main Points

1. The younger son asked his father for his share of the inheritance and then wasted it.
2. The son returned to the father to confess his sin and ask for a job as a hired worker.
3. The father restored the son's status and celebrated his return.
4. The older son was angry, but the father pleaded that he join the celebration.

The Story

Jesus welcomed tax collectors and sinners who wanted to listen to him. But Jesus's association with them made the religious leaders angry. So Jesus told a story about a father with two sons.

The younger son asked his father to divide the family inheritance and to give him his share immediately. The father did that, and the son left for another country, where he spent his entire inheritance on wild living. But then that country had a severe famine, and the son had no food. He found work caring for a farmer's pigs until he came to his senses and thought his father's workers had more than enough food and he had none. So the son returned to his father to confess he had sinned and dishonored his father and ask to be hired as one of his father's workers.

But the father saw him coming and felt compassion for him and ran to his son and immediately threw his arms around him, put his robe on him, and directed a feast with a fattened calf, saying, "My son was dead and is alive again; he was lost and now is found!" And they celebrated their reconciliation.

When the older son returned from working the fields, he heard the celebration and asked a servant what was happening, and the servant explained that his younger brother had returned. This made the older son angry, and he refused to join the celebration. The father went outside to plead with his son to join the celebration, but the son said, "All these years I've worked for you and have never disobeyed you. Yet you never gave me even a young goat to celebrate with my friends. But now my brother lost your property for women through wild living, and you killed the fatted calf for him!"

The father replied, "You are always with me, and everything I have is yours. But we have to celebrate, because your brother was dead and is now alive! He was lost, and now he's found!"

The Questions

1. Is this story about the sons or the father? Who do you believe these three characters represent?
2. Why do you think Jesus doesn't include an ending to the story?
3. What were the motivations of each son toward their father?
4. What would it personally cost the older son to respond favorably to the father?
5. Did the father give honor to both sons, whether faithful or unfaithful?

The Scripture Memory: 1 John 1:9

The Hook Question

If I believed I had insulted God, what could I do to show I now respected him, so he would give me his favor instead of his anger?

J 19: Jesus Is the Good Shepherd

The Misconceptions

- We are able to protect ourselves; we have no need of someone to protect us.
- We are unable to hear Jesus's words and teachings.
- We have no enemies who are trying to scatter us from others like us.

The Passage: John 10:1–21

The Main Points

1. Jesus is the protective gate to the sheep pen and the familiar voice to lead the sheep in and out.
2. The wolves seek to devour and scatter the sheep, but Jesus is the good shepherd who has authority to willingly lay down his life for the sheep and pick his life up again.
3. God the Father loves Jesus, because Jesus will sacrifice his life for the other sheep elsewhere.

The Story

Jesus compared his ministry to his disciples as a good shepherd. The good shepherd enters the sheep pen through the gate, but Jesus warned that robbers and thieves—who want to steal, kill, and devour the sheep—climb over the pen another way. The watchman opens the gate for the shepherd, and the sheep recognize his voice, and the shepherd calls the sheep by name and leads them out to pasture before returning them back to the pen. But the sheep will not recognize a stranger's voice and will not follow him.

The disciples didn't understand Jesus's reference as a shepherd, so Jesus explained that he was both the gate that protects the sheep and the good shepherd who would lay down his life for the sheep. A hired worker runs from dangerous wolves and leaves the sheep scattered, because he doesn't own the sheep. In comparison, the shepherd who owns the sheep is committed to them and remains to protect them even at the cost of his own life. The shepherd knows his sheep, and the sheep know his voice, and the good shepherd has come that they may have life and have it to the full.

Jesus then said, "My Father loves me, because I lay down my life for the sheep, only to take it up again. No one takes my life from me, but I lay it down by my own will. I have authority from my Father to lay my life down and authority to pick it up again. I have other sheep in another sheep pen, and I must bring them also."

The Questions

1. How do you think you could recognize the voice of Jesus as your shepherd who protects you?
2. How can a sheep protect itself from evil people who are as dangerous as wolves?
3. Is it possible to distinguish a hired worker from others who would protect the flock as good shepherds, before a crisis comes to threaten the flock?
4. How could you become a shepherd to others? What would you do differently?

The Scripture Memory: Ps 23:1–4

The Hook Questions

Who trusts me? What have I done to have them trust me?

What has Jesus done for me that I should trust him?

J 20: Jesus Is the Good Leader

The Misconceptions

- Leaders have all the power and authority to appoint other leaders.
- Great leaders should be powerful, to enforce their authority and will upon their subjects.
- Jesus will establish a political rule in his future kingdom.

The Passages: Matt 20:20–28; Mark 10:35–45

The Main Points

1. Salome and her sons asked Jesus to appoint them as leaders.
2. After asking about their willingness to suffer with him, Jesus corrected their understanding; it is God who prepares and appoints leaders.
3. The other disciples reacted angrily to James and John's arrogant appeal to lead, so Jesus taught that great leaders possess humility and servanthood to all, not authoritarian lordship.

The Story

Toward the end of Jesus's ministry, before entering Jerusalem, Salome asked Jesus if he would appoint her two sons, James and John, to be on his left and right when Jesus claimed his kingdom. James and John were Jesus's disciples, so Jesus asked them if they would be willing to drink the cup of suffering as he was about to do. They said they were able. Jesus said they would indeed suffer, but he did not have the authority to fill leadership roles, because only the Father in heaven prepared and appointed persons for leadership positions.

When the other ten disciples overheard Salome and her sons' request, they were angry. So Jesus called them together and said, "Those recognized as leaders among the non-Jews use authoritative power to rule over others. But you should not follow their example. If you want to be a great leader, you must be a servant. Whoever wants to be first must instead be servant of all. For even the Son of Man did not come to be served but to serve and to give his life as a ransom for many."

The Questions

1. Which practices do authoritarian leaders rely upon to rule over others?
2. Why would serving others be more appropriate for leaders in the kingdom?
3. By what other criteria are leaders identified and appointed, if not by servanthood?
4. After three years of ministry, why do you think the disciples didn't see the difference in how Jesus led when compared to the gentiles?

The Scripture Memory: Mark 10:45

The Hook Question

In which ways do my personal or business interactions reflect how I live in my culture or in God's kingdom?

J 21: Jesus Forgave Sins as He Healed a Paralytic

The Misconceptions

- Miracles do not prove God's involvement.
- Miracles are not evidence of God's approval.
- Miracles are dependent on personal faith and not on intercessors who have faith.

The Passages: Luke 5:17–26; Matt 9:1–8; Mark 2:1–12

The Main Points

1. Jesus healed in a crowded home, surrounded by townspeople, Pharisees, and teachers.
2. Four friends brought their paralytic friend to Jesus by opening a hole in the roof.
3. Jesus saw the faith of the friends and told the paralytic his sins were forgiven.
4. The Pharisees and teachers called Jesus a blasphemer, because only God can forgive sins.
5. Jesus asked which was easier to do—declare forgiveness or heal a paralytic—before Jesus healed the paralytic to prove his authority to forgive sins.

The Story

Jesus was healing the sick and teaching in a home. The home was crowded with local townspeople and with Pharisees and teachers of the law from nearby towns.

Four friends of a paralyzed man wanted to take their friend to Jesus for healing, but they couldn't get close because of the crowd. So they climbed up to the roof from the outside and began removing ceiling tiles to lower their friend on a pallet through the hole in the ceiling.

When Jesus saw the faith of the friends, he turned to the paralytic man and said, "Your sins are forgiven." The Pharisees and teachers said to themselves, "This man is blaspheming, for only God can forgive sins!" Jesus knew what they were thinking and said, "Why are you thinking these things? Which is easier, to say 'Your sins are forgiven' or 'Get up, take your mat and walk'? But so you know that I, the Son of Man, have authority on earth to forgive sins," Jesus turned to the paralytic and continued, "Get up, take your mat and go home."

And the man got up, picked up his mat, and walked home! And all the crowd saw this, and they praised God because they had never seen anything like this before.

The Questions

1. How do you think the Pharisees and teachers would have responded to Jesus healing the paralytic man if he had not said, "Your sins are forgiven," but proceeded to heal the man?
2. For what purpose, then, did Jesus say, "Your sins are forgiven"?
3. What surprises you about Jesus's response to the faith of friends and not the faith of the paralytic?

The Scripture Memory: John 10:38

The Hook Question

Which response would Jesus expect from me if I had witnessed any of his miracles?

J 22: Jesus Defended Healing on the Sabbath

The Misconceptions

- The highest priority in demonstrating righteousness is obedience to the law's requirements.
- Any activity of love, service, or compassion is defined as work that violates Sabbath rest.
- Holiness and righteousness are revealed by refusing any activity on the Sabbath.
- Compassion or goodness is secondary to lawful obedience.

The Passages: Matt 12:9-14; Luke 13:10-17; 14:1-6

The Main Points

1. Jesus healing a shriveled hand on the Sabbath compared to rescuing a sheep from a ditch
2. Jesus healing a woman bent over eighteen years on the Sabbath compared to leading a donkey to water
3. Jesus healing a man with severe swelling on the Sabbath compared to rescuing an ox in a well

The Story

Religious leaders considered healing to be work, and working on the Sabbath day was a violation of Jewish law. One Sabbath, Jesus entered a Jewish synagogue that included a man with a shriveled hand. The synagogue leaders asked Jesus directly, "Is it legal to heal on the Sabbath?" Jesus answered with a question, "If you had a sheep that fell into a pit on the Sabbath, wouldn't you pick it up from the pit? How much more valuable is a man than a sheep! Therefore it is lawful to do good on the Sabbath." Then Jesus healed the man's hand, but the religious Pharisees angrily left to plan how to kill Jesus.

Another time, Jesus was teaching in a synagogue that included a woman who had been bent over for eighteen years. Jesus called her forward and said, "You are free from your infirmity," and the woman straightened up and praised God. But the ruler of the synagogue was angry and told the people that there were six other days of the week when they could be healed but not to seek healing on the Sabbath. Jesus responded by calling him a hypocrite and asking if they didn't untie a donkey to lead it to water on the Sabbath. If so, why shouldn't the woman bound by Satan for eighteen years be released? The leaders were all humiliated, but the people were delighted by Jesus's response.

Another time, Jesus entered the home of a prominent Pharisee on the Sabbath. A man who suffered from various swellings was present, so Jesus asked the Pharisees and other experts in the law if they thought it was lawful to heal on the Sabbath. Nobody answered, so Jesus healed the man and sent him on his way. He asked the leaders, "If one of you had a son or an ox that fell into the well on the Sabbath, wouldn't you immediately pull him out?" But again, no one answered him.

The Questions

1. What was the highest standard of righteousness held by the Pharisees and teachers of the law?
2. What was the highest standard of righteousness demonstrated by Jesus?
3. Which two priorities of the Pharisees and teachers did Jesus disagree with, and what effect did that have?
4. Do you think the response of the Pharisees to kill Jesus was motivated by a threat to their power, their law, their system of religious control, or something else?

The Scripture Memory: Mark 2:27–28

The Hook Question

How would I think through a situation in which a response was expected from me by others that I personally thought and felt in my heart would not honor God as much?

J 23: Jesus Challenged Religious Practices

The Misconceptions
- Repeating traditional religious practices approved by religious leadership assures righteousness before God.
- Traditional religious practices always follow scriptural commands.

The Passages: Luke 5:33–35; 6:1–11; 11:37–41

The Main Points
1. Jesus's disciples didn't fast while Jesus was with them as the bridegroom.
2. Picking grain on the Sabbath to satisfy hunger was lawful, because Jesus is Lord of the Sabbath.
3. Ceremoniously washing hands doesn't clean a heart full of greed and wickedness.

The Story

Jesus and his followers were often criticized by religious leaders for violating religious practices. Jesus was once asked why the followers both of John the Baptist and of the Pharisees fasted, but Jesus's followers did not. Jesus answered, "The guests of the bridegroom cannot be made to fast while the bridegroom is with them. But they will fast when the bridegroom is taken away from them."

Another time, Jesus and his followers were walking through grain fields on a Sabbath day, and some took some grain to eat. The Pharisees said that was unlawful work, forbidden on the Sabbath. Jesus answered, referring to the time King David and his companions were very hungry and entered the house of God to eat the consecrated bread that was to be eaten only by the priests. Then Jesus declared, "The Son of Man is Lord of the Sabbath."

And another time, Jesus was invited to a Pharisee's home for a meal, but the Pharisee was surprised that Jesus didn't ceremoniously wash beforehand. Jesus noticed his surprise and said, "You Pharisees clean the outside of the cup and platter, but inside you are full of robbery and wickedness. Didn't the God who made the outside also make the inside? If you give to charity from the inside, then all things are clean for you."

Thirty Story Lessons from the Life of Jesus

The Questions

1. Why do you think the religious leaders placed great importance on following these practices?
2. How did Jesus get them to reconsider their misunderstandings? Why didn't he just ignore them?
3. Why did the religious leaders conclude Jesus and his followers weren't following God's laws, which were actually religious traditions?

The Scripture Memory: Mark 7:6–8

The Hook Questions

Is the focus of my faith on increasing my personal devotion to my religious disciplines or on growing my personal relationship to God?

Why would it matter?

J 24: Jesus Criticized Because of His Friends

The Misconceptions

- A person's righteousness is always revealed by the company the person keeps.
- Calling to spiritual repentance is only for those who are spiritually righteous.
- Keeping a pure spiritual reputation is better than being a friend to those lacking a good reputation.

The Passages: Luke 5:30–32; 7:39–40, 48; 15:1–2

The Main Points

1. Jesus was criticized by religious leaders for eating with sinners.
2. Jesus was criticized by Pharisees for allowing a sinful woman to wash and perfume his feet.
3. Jesus was criticized by religious leaders for welcoming sinners.

The Story

While walking through a town, Jesus saw Levi, a hated tax collector, and told him he was going to his home. Levi joyfully invited other tax collecting friends to a banquet to honor Jesus. Seeing all these unrighteous people, the religious leaders asked Jesus, "Why do you eat and drink with tax collectors?" Jesus answered, "It's not the healthy person who needs a doctor but those who are sick. I haven't called the righteous but sinners to repentance."

Later, a Pharisee invited Jesus to his home for a meal. While Jesus lay on his side eating the meal, a woman known for living a sinful life came from behind Jesus and wept over his feet so much that his feet were wet. She tried to dry his feet with her hair and kissed his feet before pouring perfume on them. The Pharisee thought, "If Jesus was a prophet, he would know who was touching him and what kind of woman she was."

Jesus interrupted the Pharisee's thoughts with a question. "Two men owed money to a moneylender. One owed him ten times more than the other, but neither of them could pay him back. Then the moneylender cancelled the debts of both men. Which of the men would love him more?" The Pharisee answered, "I suppose the one with the bigger cancelled debt."

Jesus said, "That's right. When I entered your house, you did not give water to wash my feet or a welcoming kiss or pour oil on my head. But she washed my feet with her tears, kissed my feet, and poured perfume on my feet. So her many sins are forgiven, because she showed much love. But the one who has been forgiven little loves little." Then Jesus turned to the woman and said, "Your sins are forgiven; your faith has saved you. Go in peace."

The Questions

1. How did the tax collector and the sinful woman respond to the care given them by Jesus? How did those responses compare to the religious leaders' response to them?
2. Which values or priorities revealed by the religious leaders were rejected by Jesus?
3. Which kind of response would you expect from others whom you forgave or with whom you shared Jesus's invitation to be forgiven?

The Scripture Memory: Matt 9:13

The Hook Question

If I were to approach Jesus right now, which kind of response or reaction would I expect from him?

J 25: Religious Leaders Tried to Trap Jesus

The Misconceptions

- Increasing personal power and influence is more important than speaking truth or doing good.
- Washing hands makes a person clean before God.

The Passages: John 15:18–19; Matt 15:1–2, 10–11, 17–19; 19:1–9; 22:15–22; 22:23–30

The Main Points

1. Topics to trap Jesus included washing before meals, divorce, taxes, and marital status after resurrection.
2. Jesus's response to each question revealed his wisdom and the ignorance of the questioners.
3. Jesus promised his followers that they would face persecution as he did.

The Story

The religious leaders wanted to trap Jesus to accuse him of being a heretic. They accused Jesus and his followers of breaking religious traditions by not washing their hands before eating. Jesus answered their accusation by saying, "What goes into a man's mouth doesn't make him unclean. It is the words of his mouth from the heart that make a man unclean. From the heart come evil thoughts of murder, adultery, sexual immorality, lies, and slander that make a man unclean."

The leaders again tried to trap Jesus, asking, "Is it lawful for a man to divorce his wife for any and every reason?" Jesus answered, "A man was to leave his mother and father and become united with his wife, and the two would become one flesh, and what God has joined together, man should not separate." The leaders answered back, "Why, then, did Moses permit divorce in the law?" Jesus answered, "It was because of the hard-heartedness of man, and except for marital unfaithfulness, a man marrying another woman commits adultery."

Again, the leaders tried to trap Jesus by asking, "Is it right to pay taxes to Caesar or not?" Jesus first questioned why they were trying to trap him but then asked them whose picture was on a coin. They answered, "Caesar."

So, Jesus replied, "Give to Caesar what belongs to Caesar, and give to God what belongs to God." They were amazed by his answers and went away.

But religious leaders who denied the resurrection still tried to trap Jesus by asking, "What if a woman was married seven times to seven brothers who all died. Which brother would she be married to at the resurrection?" Jesus answered, saying that, like the angels, there would be no marriages at the resurrection. Then Jesus challenged their unbelief in the resurrection by saying that God identified himself as the God of Abraham, Isaac, and Jacob. That is, God was not the God of the dead but of the living, who would be at the resurrection. When the crowd heard this, they were astonished, and the religious leaders were silenced.

The Questions

1. Why do you think the leaders asked about detailed issues of little importance?
2. Which kind of answers do you think the religious leaders were hoping to hear from Jesus?
3. After Jesus responded to their questions, why didn't they argue any further with him?

The Scripture Memory: Luke 5:31–32

The Hook Questions

Which questions would I expect to be asked of Jesus among my friends and religious leaders if Jesus suddenly met with us?

Which questions would I expect to be most challenging or interesting to me?

J 26: Jesus Arrested and Stood for Trial

The Misconceptions

- Jesus was unable to overcome the authority and power of both political and religious leadership.
- Jesus lost control of the situation.

The Passages: Matt 26:47–68; Mark 14:43–65; 15:6–15 Luke 22:47–53, 66–71; 23:6–25; John 18:2–24, 39

The Main Points

1. Jesus's arrest in the garden
2. Jesus before the former and present high priests, Pilate, Herod, back to Pilate
3. Pilate agreed to the mob's desire to crucify Jesus, though denying Jesus was guilty.

The Story

Jesus and his disciples were in a garden after their Passover meal when Roman soldiers, priests, and elders came with swords and clubs to arrest him. Jesus asked, "Why have you come out with swords and clubs as if I was a robber? Every day I was in the temple, but you did not come after me."

They took Jesus to Annas, a former high priest, who questioned Jesus about his disciples and his teachings. Jesus answered, "I spoke openly in the temple and the synagogue and never in secret. Why do you question me? Ask those who know what I said."

Annas sent Jesus to Caiaphas, the current high priest, who asked Jesus, "Are you the Messiah, the Son of the Blessed One?" Jesus answered, "Yes," and added, "You shall see the Son of Man sitting at the right hand of power and coming on the clouds of heaven." Caiaphas called out, "We have heard his mockery of God! There is no need for other witnesses. He must die!" So Caiaphas sent Jesus to Pontius Pilate, the Roman governor, to crucify Jesus, because Jews had no authority to carry out a death penalty.

Pilate asked Jesus, "Are you king of the Jews?" Jesus replied, "It is as you say, but my kingdom is not of this world." Pilate concluded Jesus wasn't guilty, but the accusers argued that Jesus had been stirring up trouble since he began in Galilee. When Pilate heard Jesus was from Galilee, he sent Jesus to Herod, who ruled Galilee. Herod also found Jesus innocent of any crimes and returned him to Pilate.

Pilate tried another plan to release Jesus, using a Jewish custom at Passover to release a prisoner. So he asked, "Shall I release Barabbas?"— a robber and murderer. But the crowd called to crucify Jesus, and Pilate asked, "Why? And they said, "Because he made himself out to be the Son of God!"

Then Pilate asked Jesus where he was from, but Jesus gave no answer. Pilate said, "Don't you know I have authority to release or crucify you?" Jesus replied, "You have no authority over me unless that power was given to you from above."

Pilate again asked the crowd if he should crucify the one they called King of the Jews, but they answered, "We have no king except Caesar!" Pilate repeated that he found Jesus innocent but would have Jesus severely punished and then released. But the crowd still wanted Jesus crucified. Pilate had a water basin brought to him, in which he washed his hands and said, "I am innocent of this man's blood," and then released Barabbas and delivered Jesus to be crucified to satisfy the crowd.

The Questions

1. Which actions revealed the desires of the priests, Pilate, Herod, and Jesus?
2. Why do you think Jesus was still in control of the situation?
3. What was the legal charge of the priests against Jesus? Was the charge accurate?

The Scripture Memory: John 12:27

The Hook Questions

Which answer do I think each political and religious leader hoped to hear from Jesus?

Which answer would I have wanted to hear from which question if I had been there?

J 27: Jesus Tortured, Crucified, and Killed

The Misconceptions

- Jesus did not die on the cross but caused an illusion for another to die in his place.
- Jesus was executed quickly.
- Jesus was executed privately under Roman control.

The Passages: Matt 27:27–66; Mark 15:16–47; Luke 23:26–56; John 19:17–42

The Main Points

1. The whipping, crosspiece carrying, and nailing to the cross
2. The first three hours of the soldiers and chief priests mocking Jesus
3. The last three hours in darkness and agony and Jesus's last words

The Story

Pilate sentenced Jesus to be tortured and then crucified. The guards beat him, pushed thorns into his head like a crown, and whipped him, ripping his skin open. Jesus was then forced to carry the crosspiece of his cross until he was too weak to continue and soldiers called another man to carry it to the place of execution.

At nine a.m., they nailed his hands to the crosspiece and his feet to the post. He hung there for the next six hours under the soldiers' constant watch. The chief priests and rulers came by, mocking Jesus and saying, "He saved others; let him save himself if he is the Messiah. If he came down from the cross, we would believe in him." John; Mary, the mother of Jesus; and three other women were the only followers of Jesus at the cross who stood watch as Jesus died on that post.

After three hours, the sky turned dark and the sun could not be seen. Jesus told John from the cross to take his mother Mary and be responsible for her as if she were John's mother. Another three hours later, Jesus said, "I am thirsty," and a guard gave him a sponge of sour wine. But then Jesus called out, "It is finished!" and cried out, "Father, into your hands I commit my spirit!" He took his last breath and died.

Thirty Story Lessons from the Life of Jesus

The Questions

1. Why do you think Jesus was not quickly killed but forced to endure long suffering and agony—all under God's control?
2. Who, representing the political and religious powers, went to watch and mock Jesus publicly and wanted to see Jesus dead? What did they personally have at stake to be sure Jesus was dead?
3. Do you think Jesus could have stopped his own death at any time due to either his will or his power?

The Scripture Memory: Matt 27:54

The Hook Questions

Would I have wanted to stop Jesus's suffering on the cross?

If so, why? If not, which benefit would the extent of his suffering be to me if he was suffering to pay the penalty of death for my sins?

J 28: Confirmation of Jesus's Death and Burial

The Misconceptions

- Life in Jerusalem continued normally when Jesus died on the cross.
- Events that happened when Jesus died were seen by only a few and can all be explained away.
- Jesus's dead body was hidden by the disciples who then reported that Jesus had risen.

The Passages: Matt 27:51–54; 57–66; Mark 15:38–39; Luke 23:44–48; John 19:31–42

The Main Points

1. The soldiers confirmed Jesus was dead.
2. The temple curtain was torn from top to bottom; the sky turned dark.
3. Jesus's body was buried in Joseph's tomb, which was sealed, and a Roman guard was set.

The Story

Sunset was coming, which marked the start of the holy Sabbath, and a dead body could not remain on the cross during the Sabbath. When necessary, the soldiers could speed up death on the cross by breaking the legs of the person so they could no longer push their bodies up to breathe and would suffocate. But when they came to Jesus, they discovered he was already dead. A soldier pierced Jesus's side, and both blood and water came out of the wound, proving he was dead. The centurion Roman guard who saw Jesus die said, "Truly this was the Son of God. And this man was innocent."

When Jesus died, the very tall curtain that separated the holiest place within the Jerusalem temple and prevented anyone from seeing into the room was immediately torn in two from the top to the bottom. This holiest place was entered only once a year by the high priest, but now the entrance to the room was open. At the same time, there was also an earthquake, and tombs were opened, and many of the dead were raised to life, which was seen by the inhabitants of Jerusalem.

Joseph, a member of the Jewish Council who believed in Jesus, asked Pilate for Jesus's body to place in his own tomb. Pilate approved his request, and the body was placed in the tomb, where the women wrapped the body with a mixture of spices according to the Jewish custom.

The chief priests and leaders returned to Pilate and asked for guards to stand watch over the tomb to make certain Jesus's followers wouldn't try to steal the body and say Jesus was still alive. Pilate agreed to the guard and had a Roman seal placed over the tombstone to ensure the body wouldn't be stolen.

The Questions

1. What would you be thinking if there were an earthquake with great darkness?
2. Do you think the temple veil being torn from the top to the bottom or the graves of holy people being opened would be more convincing that spiritual power was revealed?
3. How many people confirmed Jesus's death?

The Scripture Memory: Mark 15:39

The Hook Questions

Which motivations of the Roman guards would encourage them not to certify the death of Jesus?

Why would they want to prove it correctly?

J 29: Jesus Resurrected from Burial Tomb

The Misconceptions

- Jesus's body was stolen and hidden by Jesus's followers, who then created the myth of the resurrection.
- The nature of Jesus's resurrected body was the same one as the body that had just been killed on the cross.

The Passages: Matt 28:1–15; Mark 16:1–19; Luke 24:1–51; John 20:1–29

The Main Points

1. The guarded tomb
2. The discovery of the empty tomb
3. The announcement by the angels
4. The cover-up by the guards

The Story

Jesus died midafternoon Friday. His body was wrapped and placed in a tomb with a large stone rolled in front of the entrance and then sealed and guarded by Roman guards before Sabbath began at sunset. It was early Sunday morning when four women who had followed Jesus came to his tomb to anoint his body with spices for burial. They talked on the way about who they would ask to move the stone for them. But a second earthquake had struck during the night, and an angel had moved the stone and then sat upon it. This had frightened the guards so much they had fled.

So when the women arrived, they found the tomb open, but Jesus's body was missing. The burial linens wrapped around Jesus were now folded, the facecloth folded separately and placed above the linens. While the women were confused, two angels appeared and asked them, "Why do you seek the living among the dead? Jesus is not here; he has risen! Go and tell his disciples to meet Jesus in Galilee as he told them earlier." So the women ran back to the disciples and reported everything, but it sounded like nonsense to them, but Peter and John ran to the tomb to see it themselves. When they arrived and saw the linens, they believed Jesus was resurrected, but they didn't understand what it meant, and they returned to Jerusalem.

Meanwhile, the guards reported what had happened to the chief priests, who gave them much money to say the disciples came at night and stole the body while they were sleeping. The priests promised to win over King Herod if he were to hear of their failure to guard the tomb.

Mary Magdalene returned to the tomb crying. She saw someone she thought was the gardener. She asked if he knew where the body had been taken, but the man replied by calling her by name. She recognized it was Jesus, and she grabbed and worshipped him. He told her to tell the others. He was yet to rise to his Father but would first meet them in Galilee.

The Questions

1. Which clues in the story indicate the resurrection was unexpected by the disciples? Why would this help confirm the disciples were not involved in Jesus's resurrection? If they were involved in the resurrection, how would their statements and behaviors be different to create a different story?
2. How does Jesus's ability to either appear or disappear from sight influence your conclusions about the nature of Jesus's resurrected body?
3. Why do you think the guards risked reporting to the priests and not to the Roman authorities?

The Scripture Memory: Matt 28:5–6

The Hook Question

Are the interactions with the Romans, the angels, or the women the most convincing and influential to me about the resurrection?

J 30: Jesus Ascended to Heaven

The Misconceptions

- Only Jesus's disciples testified they saw the resurrected Jesus.
- Jesus appeared only immediately after his resurrection.
- Jesus's resurrection was only his spirit and not his physical body.

The Passages: Luke 24:13–32; Matt 28:1–15; John 20:11–18; Acts 1:3–11; 1 Cor 15:6–7

The Main Points

1. Jesus's appearances to the women
2. Jesus's appearance on the road to Emmaus
3. Jesus's appearance to the disciples in the room
4. Jesus appeared to others for forty days before giving his last commission to his disciples and ascending to heaven.

The Story

Mary was the first to see Jesus resurrected at the tomb, accompanied by two other women who saw angels in the empty tomb who announced Jesus had risen from the dead. They reported Jesus had risen to the eleven disciples, but the disciples refused to believe them.

That afternoon, as two disciples walked to a town called Emmaus, they were joined by Jesus, who they couldn't recognize. Jesus asked what they were talking about. One answered, "Are you the only one visiting Jerusalem and unaware of the things that have happened?" Jesus asked, "What things?" They answered, "Three days ago, Jesus, a mighty prophet in word and works, was crucified by the chief priests and rulers. We had hoped he was the one to redeem Israel. But this morning, some of our women went to his tomb, and it was empty. But then they saw Jesus and a vision of angels who said he was alive!"

Jesus said, "You are foolish and slow to believe," and beginning with Moses and all the prophets, taught them how all these sufferings were necessary to be accomplished by the Messiah before his being glorified. It was getting late, and the disciples urged him to stay with them overnight. He ate dinner with them, and as soon as Jesus blessed the bread, they recognized him, and Jesus immediately disappeared.

That same night, the eleven disciples were together, fearing for their lives in a locked room. Jesus suddenly appeared in the room and said, "Peace be with you. Why are your hearts troubled? Touch me and see, for a spirit does not have flesh and bones as you see I have. Do you have anything to eat?" And they gave him broiled fish, which he ate before them.

For the next forty days, Jesus appeared many more times to the disciples, including eating with them by the Galilean seashore. He taught them more about the kingdom of God, but he also met and was seen by many others, including over five hundred people at one time. And then, on Mount Olivet outside Jerusalem, he told them they would receive power when the Holy Spirit came upon them, and they would be Jesus's witnesses in Jerusalem, Judah, and Samaria, to the farthest parts of the world. And then he blessed them before rising up in the sky until a cloud blocked him from their sight.

The Questions

1. Which incidents in the story indicate the resurrection was unexpected to the disciples?
2. Which of Jesus's actions convince you of Jesus's bodily resurrection?
3. What was so important for Jesus to be seen for forty days to hundreds of people? What did Jesus hope to accomplish with his disciples and with hundreds of others' witnesses?

The Scripture Memory: Acts 1:8

The Hook Question

What would make my own witness of Jesus's resurrection as persuasive as the first-century witnesses?

Chapter 4

Thirty New Testament Story Lessons

NT 1: The Holy Spirit Arrived on Pentecost

The Misconceptions

- Speaking in an unknown foreign language is not a miraculous sign, because it can be explained naturally.
- The disciples could not prove or give an explanation to confirm these new events.

The Passages: Acts 1:8; 2:1–41

The Main Points

1. Jesus commanded the disciples to wait in Jerusalem for the baptism of the Holy Spirit.
2. The Holy Spirit baptism appeared as fire and enabled them to speak in foreign languages.
3. Peter used Scripture of Joel and King David to explain the events.
4. The people responded in repentance and baptism.

The Story

Before Jesus entered heaven after his resurrection, he commanded his disciples to stay in Jerusalem and wait for the baptism of the Holy Spirit and the Spirit's power. They remained together in one room and prayed for ten days. Jerusalem was filled with Jews from every nation and language, celebrating the harvest begun fifty days earlier during Passover. The celebration was called "Pentecost," which was the Greek word for "fifty."

Suddenly, the sound of a violent wind filled the room, and a flame appeared, which became a single flame over each disciple. Each of the disciples began to talk in a foreign language unknown to them. When the disciples left the room, the foreign visitors in Jerusalem were amazed to hear these men speak in their homeland language. Local Jews said they had been drinking too much wine, but the disciple Peter spoke to the crowd, saying no one was drinking wine because it was only nine in the morning.

Then Peter spoke from the prophet Joel, who wrote hundreds of years ago, "I will pour out my Spirit in those days, and they will prophesy." Then Peter spoke from a psalm of David, in which God promised he would not abandon him to the grave and his body would not decay. But Peter said, "King David's body is still here and decayed in the grave, so the promise must be for another. Jesus was killed and buried, but his body did not remain in the grave, and his body has not decayed. Jesus, who you killed, was God's promised Lord and Messiah."

When the crowd heard this, they were overwhelmed and saddened and called out to Peter, "What should we do?" Peter warned them and said they had to repent, change their minds about Jesus, and be baptized in Jesus's name. That day, three thousand people were baptized as followers of Jesus.

The Questions

1. Why did the crowd so quickly choose drunkenness to explain speaking in different languages?
2. Which evidence did Peter rely upon that was stronger than the crowd's explanation of drunkenness?
3. Why didn't the crowd argue that Jesus's body was still in the tomb?

The Scripture Memory: 1 Cor 14:22

The Hook Questions

If I witnessed something I couldn't explain, how would I describe what I saw to another?

Why might I be reluctant to use supernatural explanations?

NT 2: A Lame Man Was Healed in the Name of Jesus

The Misconceptions

- Financial support is the primary need of the physically disabled.
- Power and intimidation can overcome contrary facts.
- Personal spiritual power and godliness enable healing of the sick.

The Passage: Acts 3:1—4:31

The Main Points

1. The beggar, crippled from birth, begged daily at the Temple Gate.
2. The beggar was healed by the command of Peter in the name of Jesus Christ.
3. The religious courts threatened Peter and John against speaking in Jesus's name.
4. The disciples were released, and five thousand men believed in their testimony about Jesus.

The Story

For over forty years, a man crippled from birth begged daily for money at the gate to the Jerusalem temple. One afternoon, the disciples Peter and John walked by him on their way to prayers, and he asked them for money. Peter looked directly at him and said, "I have no silver or gold, but what I do have I give to you. In the name of Jesus, get up and walk!" Peter helped him get up, and he took a few steps and then leaped and danced in joy!

The crowd looked at him and then at Peter, who said, "Why are you surprised? Why are you looking at us as if it was our own spiritual power or godliness that made this happen? God chose to glorify Jesus, whom you disowned and killed. But it's in his name—and no other—that this man was strengthened and healed. I know you and your leaders acted in ignorance when you killed Jesus. But this man was healed by faith in Jesus's name. You must repent and turn to God so your sins can be wiped away."

The growing crowd attracted the priests, the captain of the temple guard, and the Sadducees, who put Peter and John in the prison overnight for preaching about Jesus's resurrection. But many believed Peter, and the number of those who repented and turned to follow Jesus grew to five thousand men.

The next day, Peter and John were brought before all the religious leaders and priests, who asked by which power or name did they perform this miracle. Peter told them it was by the name of Jesus whom they had crucified and rejected. But the proof of the crippled man now standing by Peter and John didn't allow the leaders and priests to deny what had happened, so they ordered Peter and John not to speak or teach again in Jesus's name. Peter responded asking them to judge for themselves whether it was right in God's sight to obey them rather than God. The leaders didn't answer the challenge but just continued to threaten them further, because they couldn't decide how to punish them.

The Questions

1. Compare the results the crippled man and Peter were expecting when they first met at the temple gate. Would those results have been satisfying to each of them? Which additional results did God want?
2. Why would Peter require the use of Jesus's name and no other to see the power of the Holy Spirit?
3. What prevented the religious leaders from getting the response they hoped for by threatening Peter and John?

The Scripture Memory: Acts 3:16

The Hook Question

If I had the spiritual gift to heal sicknesses, would I be motivated to use the gift to reduce suffering, to bring glory to God, or to bring attention to the concerns and issues that were important to me?

NT 3: Man and Wife Lied to the Holy Spirit

The Misconceptions

- Gaining honor and respect is a priority, even if misrepresentation or deception is used.
- God can be deceived.
- God does not know or challenge my personal wealth or amount I choose to give to others.
- God judges people according to the amount they chose to give.

The Passage: Acts 5:1–11

The Main Points

1. No needy people in the church because of sharing and donations from land and homeowners
2. Ananias and Sapphira sold their land and lied about the amount they received and donated.
3. Ananias was challenged by Peter, who declared Ananias hadn't lied to men but to God, and Ananias died.
4. Sapphira went to Peter and also lied about the amount, and she died.
5. Fear gripped the church because of the judgments.

The Story

The early church shared what they had with other believers, so no one was needy. Followers who were homeowners or landowners would, from time to time, sell off some land or homes and give the money to the apostles to distribute to those in need.

Ananias and his wife, Sapphira, owned much land. They decided to sell and declare they were giving all the profits of the sale to the apostles, though they secretly planned to keep some of the money for themselves. When Ananias laid the money at the foot of Peter, Peter challenged Ananias, asking him, "How has Satan so filled your heart that you would lie to the Holy Spirit and keep some of the money for yourself from the land? Didn't it belong to you before you sold it? And after you sold it, didn't the money belong to you? What made you think of doing such a thing? You haven't lied to man but to God!" After Ananias heard Peter, he fell down dead, and young men carried his body out for burial.

Three hours later, Sapphira came to Peter. She did not know her husband had died when Peter had exposed his deceitfulness. So Peter asked Sapphira, "Was this the amount you and Ananias got for the land?" And Sapphira said, "Yes, that's the price." And Peter said, "How could you agree to test the Spirit of the Lord? These are the men who just buried your husband, and now they will take you out also." And Sapphira fell at Peter's feet and died. And the whole church responded with reverent fear before God.

The Questions

1. What motivated Ananias and Sapphira to describe their gift as a total sacrifice rather than a partial donation made possible by the sale?
2. How do you think Peter learned of Ananias's deception?
3. What did Ananias and Sapphira fail to understand about God or the church that allowed them to think they were deceiving only their spiritual family?

The Scripture Memory: Prov 21:2; Matt 9:4

The Hook Questions

What would I sacrifice to receive increased respect and honor among my friends?

What would tempt me to deceive others to increase my reputation?

NT 4: Jews Persecuted Stephen to His Death

The Misconceptions

- Authorities can affect God's plans, using persecution through mobs, intimidation, jail, and even death.
- Persecution and fear reduce the number of believers and commitment level of those believers oppressed.

The Passages: Acts 5:17-42; 7:54—8:5, 14-17

The Main Points

1. Imprisoned ministering disciples released by angel, who commanded they continue to preach
2. Stephen stoned to death, beginning increased persecution of believers
3. Disciples fled from persecution. Philip fled to Samaria, began a church, and baptized believers. Peter and John placed their hands on the Samaritans, who were baptized by the Holy Spirit.

The Story

After Peter healed the crippled man in Jesus's name at the temple gate, other disciples taught and healed on the temple grounds. The crowds grew so large that the religious leaders put all the disciples in prison overnight. But during the night, an angel of the Lord opened the prison doors and told them to continue to preach at the temple.

The next morning, the religious leaders wanted to question the disciples and directed the guards to bring the disciples to them. But the guards returned, saying the jail doors were still locked, but the disciples were gone, and other guards reported the disciples were at the temple preaching.

The disciples were brought back to court. The leaders demanded they were not to teach in Jesus's name, but the disciples replied they had to obey God and not men. This made the leaders so angry they wanted to kill them all. But one of their teachers reminded them that others had tried to start a movement, and it had come to nothing. He said, "Either this movement will also come to nothing, or you could be trying to fight God." So the leaders whipped the disciples, commanded them again not to teach in Jesus's name, and let them go.

But they continued to teach, heal, and perform signs to support their message. Stephen, a godly teacher, frustrated Jewish leaders because of his wisdom and godliness, and some Jews stirred up the crowd by falsely accusing him of blasphemy. Before the high priest, Stephen gave a history of Jewish disobedience and rebellion against the prophets, which so angered the Jews, he was stoned to death.

Saul, a Pharisee, was at the stoning of Stephen. He went to every house and imprisoned any believers. The disciples scattered from Jerusalem. Philip, an evangelist, went to Samaria and saw many Samaritans believe in Jesus. He then baptized them. When Peter and John heard of this great response to Philip's preaching, they traveled to Samaria to investigate. When they placed their hands on the heads of Samaritan believers, the Holy Spirit baptized the Samaritans with the same result as the disciples experienced at Pentecost. So the church expanded from Jerusalem to Samaria.

The Questions

1. What motivated the Jewish leaders to increase their persecution by commanding and warning Peter and John; then by commanding, jailing, and whipping all the disciples; and then finally murdering Stephen?
2. What did the Jewish leaders hope would result from their intimidation, jailing, whippings, and stoning?
3. How did the religious persecution from the Jewish leaders encourage the growth and spread of the gospel?

The Scripture Memory: 2 Tim 3:12

The Hook Question

Are there any reasons I would risk identifying myself with those being persecuted for their faith?

NT 5: Saul, a Persecutor, Converted by Jesus

The Misconceptions

- Persecutors are so committed they will never change their minds.
- God calls to lead others only those who have proven their loyalty to him and service to others.
- Those God chooses to lead others are protected from suffering and greatly blessed.

The Passage: Acts 9:1–25

The Main Points

1. Gospel and persecution spread
2. Saul was blinded and heard Jesus question his persecution on road to Damascus
3. Saul and Ananias received visions to heal his blindness
4. Saul was baptized, preached Jesus, and escaped from Damascus

The Story

Saul, a Pharisee, approved Stephen's death by stoning. The high priest gave authority to Saul to go beyond Jerusalem and arrest Jewish men and women who supported Jesus's teachings and return them to Jerusalem for imprisonment.

When Saul approached Damascus, a light from heaven flashed around him, and he fell to the ground and heard a voice asking, "Saul, why are you persecuting me?" Saul asked, "Who are you, Lord?" And the voice answered, "I am Jesus, whom you are persecuting. Now go into the city and you will be told what to do."

The men accompanying Saul heard a sound but not as words. When Saul opened his eyes, he couldn't see, so they guided him into the city. He went to a house and did not eat or drink anything for three days. Then he received a vision that a man named Ananias would place his hands on him and his sight would be restored.

The Lord also gave a vision to Ananias to go to that house and ask for Saul. Ananias knew how dangerous Saul was and told the Lord that Saul had authority to arrest and imprison believers. But the Lord answered that

Saul was his chosen person to take the gospel to the gentiles, and he would also stand before kings and Israelites and suffer much for him.

So Ananias went to the house and placed his hands on Saul. Something like scales fell from Saul's eyes, and he could see again. Ananias baptized him, and Saul regained his strength and began to preach and prove from the Scriptures that Jesus was the Messiah.

The Questions

1. What motivated Saul to persecute followers of Jesus? Were his motivations wrong?
2. Why should persecuted believers be encouraged that Jesus views their persecution so personally and that persecuting believers is persecuting him?
3. What changed in Saul so he could argue powerfully that Jesus was the Christ?
4. Which attributes caused Jesus to choose Saul, even while Saul was persecuting him to spread the gospel?
5. Jesus chose Saul to stand before kings but also to suffer for him. Can good come from persecution?

The Scripture Memory: Acts 22:14–15

The Hook Question

Can my highest levels of sincerity and commitment overcome a wrong judgment?

NT 6: Saul's Conversion Met with Disbelief

The Misconceptions

- Observing the past actions of people justifies anticipating their future response.
- People don't change lifetime commitments to their beliefs.
- Expectations of future events are built upon past events.

The Passage: Acts 9:19–32

The Main Points

1. Saul preached and argued among the Jews in Damascus, who began planning to kill him.
2. Saul returned to Jerusalem and argued persuasively among the Jews who tried to kill him.
3. Saul was pushed away by the disciples and sent back to his home in Tarsus, resulting in the churches enjoying peace and growth.

The Story

After Saul regained his sight and his strength, he spent many days with the disciples in Damascus. Saul began preaching about Jesus in the synagogues. Many of the Jews couldn't believe it was the same man who had persecuted believers in Jerusalem and had now came to arrest believers in Damascus to imprison in Jerusalem. His message so angered the Jews, they planned to kill him. To help him escape, the believers put Saul in a basket and lowered him outside the city wall.

Saul safely made his way back to Jerusalem and began preaching and debating fearlessly in the synagogues. But the apostles didn't trust him and feared getting near him. However, one influential believer, Barnabas, believed Saul had truly changed, and he repeated the story of how Jesus met Saul on the road, giving Saul some credibility among the believers. When the Jews again tried to kill Saul, the Christian brothers took him to the coast and put him on a ship to his hometown, Tarsus, for his own protection. After Saul left, all the churches in Judea, Galilee, and Samaria grew large, and they enjoyed peace from persecution.

Thirty New Testament Story Lessons

The Questions

1. How was the Jews' response to Saul's new beliefs different than the response of believers?
2. Why didn't the believers trust Saul had changed as they had experienced change after they believed in Jesus?
3. Which help did Saul need to receive acceptance, including trust and forgiveness, from the Christians?

The Scripture Memory: Acts 9:27

The Hook Questions

Would my past actions shape others' opinions or expectations from me in the future, after I had made personal changes?

What would cause others to either trust me or disbelieve me?

NT 7: Phillip Led by the Spirit to an Ethiopian

The Misconceptions

- Successful ministry is defined by counting the number of new believers.
- Unsuccessful ministry outreach is a result of only one new believer.
- A single person from a different race from a foreign country is not a fruitful ministry objective.

The Passages: Acts 8:5–8, 25–40

The Main Points

1. Philip's responsive and broad ministry in Samaria
2. The angel's direction to a single, spiritually curious person from a different race and region on a wilderness road
3. The power of the word of God and a single spirit-filled evangelist

The Story

Philip was an evangelist who fled Jerusalem's persecution to minister in Samaria. His ministry was very successful as he preached about Jesus, cast out demons, and healed people in the name of Jesus. Afterwards, Philip planned to return north to Jerusalem and continue to minister in his travels.

But an angel of the Lord spoke to Philip and told him to go further south on a road through the wilderness to Gaza. So Philip went to the road and saw an Ethiopian official in a chariot. The angel told Philip to join the chariot. The official was very influential, as he oversaw the treasury of the queen mother and was returning home from worshipping in Jerusalem. He had a scroll of Israel's prophet Isaiah.

The official invited Philip to join him in the chariot. The passage of Scripture he was reading was "He was led as a sheep to the slaughter and, like a lamb was silent. And in his humiliation, his life was taken and removed from the earth." And the official asked Philip: "Please tell me who the prophet was referring to; himself or another?"

So Philip began with that prophecy and preached about Jesus to him. As they continued traveling, they came to some water, and the official asked Philip, "Here's water! What prevents me from being baptized?" And Philip replied, "If you believe with all your heart, you may." And the official answered, "I believe that Jesus Christ is the Son of God." So they stopped, and Philip baptized the official, and when they came out of the water, the Spirit of God had snatched Philip away to another city, but the official joyfully continued his trip home.

The Questions

1. How did the Ethiopian reveal his spiritual hunger and learning attitude?
2. Does it seem surprising to you that the angel would direct Philip away from a large and responsive group of Samaritans to meet one person in the wilderness from a different race and region?
3. After hearing and understanding the word of God explained by a teacher with the Holy Spirit, and giving a testimony of his faith in Jesus Christ, what was the next response of the Ethiopian?
4. What do you think the Ethiopian did when he arrived back in his homeland?

The Scripture Memory: Acts 1:8

The Hook Questions

Is there any place I can go where I would not be able to depend upon the Holy Spirit to give me the power to tell a story about Jesus?

Can I depend on the Holy Spirit to defend me?

NT 8: Peter Led by the Spirit to Roman Gentiles

The Misconceptions

- The benefits of Jesus's messiahship are only for Jews but irrelevant to gentiles.
- Personal righteousness is based upon avoiding all unclean actions.
- God doesn't need man to tell his revelation; he can fully reveal himself by himself.

The Passage: Acts 10:1—11:18

The Main Points

1. God responded to Cornelius's prayers through an angel and then prepared Peter through a vision.
2. While Peter presented the gospel, the Holy Spirit baptized the gentile believers as he had at Pentecost.
3. Peter reported the details of the events to Jewish believers in Jerusalem who then praised God.

The Story

Cornelius, a Roman centurion, was a righteous man who respected the Jews, gave to the poor, and regularly offered prayers. One afternoon, he saw a vision of an angel who told him that God had noticed his prayers and offerings and wanted Cornelius to send men to bring a man named Simon Peter to his home. The angel gave detailed instructions how to find Simon Peter in a neighboring town. Cornelius sent three men to the house.

The next day at noon, while Peter was praying, he had a vision of a sheet lowered from heaven filled with unclean animals, reptiles, and birds, and he heard a voice say, "Kill and eat!" Peter replied, "Certainly not! I have never eaten anything impure or unclean." The voice answered Peter, "Do not call anything impure that God has made clean." This vision happened three times. Peter reflected on it until he heard men asking for him at the door. The men said their master, Cornelius, was told by an angel to bring him back to Cornelius's home to hear what he had to say. Peter and six other believers left with them.

When Peter arrived, he told Cornelius it was against Jewish law for a Jew to visit or associate with a gentile, but God had just shown him that he should not call anything impure or unclean that God had cleansed. So Peter entered the room which Cornelius had filled with his family and friends.

Peter said, "I now realize God does not show favoritism but accepts men from every nation who fear him and do what is right." And he began telling them about the life, ministry, death, and resurrection of Jesus and of receiving forgiveness of sins through Jesus's name. While he was speaking, the Holy Spirit baptized everyone as he had the disciples at Pentecost, and the gentiles now also spoke in foreign languages that were unknown to them. Peter asked, "Can anyone keep these people from being baptized with water now that they've been baptized by the Spirit?" And everyone was baptized in the name of Jesus.

When Peter returned to Jerusalem, the Jewish believers criticized Peter for going to the home of a gentile and eating with them. When he told them of the baptism of the Holy Spirit, those who had objected now praised God, saying, "So God has even granted gentiles repentance unto life."

The Questions

1. What do you think gave Peter confidence in his own righteousness before the trance? How did his self-righteousness change after he discovered God rejected favoritism?
2. Why didn't the angel tell Cornelius the gospel and, instead, rely upon Peter to tell him?
3. How would Peter have responded to Cornelius's request if he had not had the vision first?

The Scripture Memory: Acts 10:34–35; Rom 9:30–31

The Hook Questions

Based upon past experiences, beliefs, and responses, who among my friends would I least expect to accept these stories about God and Jesus?

Can God overrule those reactions?

NT 9: Peter Led by the Spirit Out of a Prison

The Misconceptions

- The government determines who will be persecuted, prosecuted, punished, and killed.
- The government is more powerful than believers' prayers.

The Passage: Acts 12:1–19

The Main Points

1. King Herod persecuted the church, killing James and arresting Peter, intending to execute him.
2. Herod appointed four squads of four soldiers to guard Peter as the church prayed for Peter's release.
3. An angel freed Peter of his chains and led him out the prison doors before vanishing.
4. Peter went to the house church and then left the city that night. The guards were executed by Herod.

The Story

King Herod Agrippa began to persecute the church again. He arrested and executed James, the brother of John, who led the church. When he saw the Jews were happy with his action, he arrested Peter and was waiting until Passover ended before holding a public trial that would presumably end with Peter's execution. Herod doubled the jail security by assigning four squads of four soldiers each; two would be chained to Peter and the other two would guard the gate.

It was the last night of Passover before the trial. The church was gathered together praying for Peter's release. The guards were at their posts and chained to Peter, who was soundly asleep.

Suddenly an angel was in the cell. He struck Peter on the side to awaken him and told him to get up. When he did, the chains fell off Peter, and the angel told him to put on his clothes and sandals and follow him. They passed the first gate. Then the second gate leading to the city opened by itself. They walked the length of the outside street, and the angel vanished. That's when Peter realized he wasn't just seeing a vision, but his escape was real.

Peter went to the home of Mary, John Mark's mother, where the church met. They were praying for Peter's release. Peter knocked on the outer gate door, and the servant girl, Rhoda, answered it. But when she recognized Peter's voice, she didn't open the door but rushed to announce to the others that Peter was at the door, leaving Peter still outside. They thought she was out of her mind, but she insisted it was him. So they believed it was Peter's ghost. Meanwhile, Peter continued knocking until they finally let him in and were astonished as Peter described the night's events. He then told them to tell James, the half-brother of Jesus, and the other brothers. He then escaped from Jerusalem to go to another place that night.

The next morning, the guards had no explanation where Peter might be. Herod himself interviewed the guards and then had them executed for allowing the prisoner Peter to escape.

The Questions

1. Which differences are revealed between Herod's actions of insecurity and Peter's actions on his last night before his trial and likely execution?
2. How did the church indicate their astonishment that their prayers were answered?
3. James was martyred, and Peter was rescued. Does that reflect differences in power or purpose? How did the power and purpose guide the responses of the church to God and to the king?

The Scripture Memory: Prov 21:1

The Hook Question

If I were persecuted, would my prayers be more focused on hope, escape, and release or on expecting continued persecution? Why?

NT 10: Persecution Scattered the Jerusalem Believers

The Misconceptions
- Miracles always lead to belief.
- Believers can independently teach and organize ministry without accountability to the church.
- When God sets you aside from one ministry, start your own ministry.

The Passages: Acts 11:19–26; 13:1–3

The Main Points
1. Persecution caused the ministry to grow in Antioch.
2. Barnabas recruited Saul of Tarsus to teach with him for a year.
3. The Lord directed the church to release Barnabas and Saul to a new ministry but with accountability to their church.
4. Barnabas and Saul traveled to Crete, confronted a false prophet who was blinded, and saw the conversion of the Roman governor.

The Story

Persecution scattered the Jerusalem believers to other cities. Many believers traveled north to Antioch where they told about Jesus. So many Antiochians became believers that they were first called Christians in Antioch. When reports of the large number of new believers reached Jerusalem, the Jerusalem church sent godly Barnabas to Antioch and evaluate the work.

Barnabas had first supported Saul in Jerusalem before Saul was sent to his hometown of Tarsus. But Barnabas recognized the great need for teaching so he went to Tarsus to find Saul and brought him back into ministry at Antioch. They taught together for a full year until the Holy Spirit directed the church leadership of Antioch to release Barnabas and Saul for other work He had for them. So the church fasted, prayed, placed their hands on them and sent them off with John Mark.

They first went to Crete and traveled to a city where Elymas, a Jewish sorcerer and false prophet, served the Roman governor. The Roman governor wanted to hear from Barnabas and Saul, who used the name Paul when among the gentiles.

Elymas tried to turn the governor against Barnabas and Paul, but Paul, full of the Holy Spirit, looked Elymas in the eye and said, "You are a child of the devil. You are full of deceit. Will you never stop perverting the right ways of the Lord? The hand of God is against you and you are going to be blind for a while." Elymas immediately became blind. Seeing this, the governor believed the teaching from Paul and Barnabas.

The Questions

1. What do you think Paul's first reactions might have been when Barnabas asked him to minister with him in Antioch?
2. God didn't directly call Barnabas and Paul to leave on their own, but directed the leadership of a very young church to direct Barnabas and Paul. What does this teach about God's view of the church and about accountability?
3. Compare Paul being sent away earlier from Jerusalem to Tarsus with being sent away by the Antioch leaders. Which different results in attitude or effectiveness could result from each event?

The Scripture Memory: Acts 11:25–26

The Hook Questions

Who would I hope to support and encourage me if I believed I should tell others these stories?

Whom could I pray for, to come alongside me?

NT 11: Persecution Directed Paul to Other Cities

The Misconceptions

- Miracles always accurately interpret God's revelation and confirm his authority.
- Crowds slowly reach reasoned conclusions and remain consistent in their blessings or condemnations.
- Listeners always decide about Christianity slowly and deliberately.

The Passage: Acts 14:1–20

The Main Points

1. At Iconium, some believed Paul and Barnabas, but non-believing Jews and gentiles tried to kill them, so they fled to Lystra.
2. At Lystra, a crippled man believed and was healed, so the crowds believed Paul and Barnabus were gods, but enemies from Antioch and Iconium turned the mob against them, and they stoned Paul, believing him dead.
3. The disciples recovered Paul and ministered to him before he left Lystra the next morning.

The Story

Barnabas and Paul traveled to the city of Iconium to speak at the local synagogue. God confirmed their messages about Jesus with signs and wonders, but Jews who disbelieved them joined non-believing gentiles to try to kill them. To avoid further persecution, Paul and Barnabas fled to the city of Lystra.

At Lystra, as Paul preached, he saw a man with crippled feet come to faith in Jesus as he listened. Paul looked directly at the crippled man and commanded, "Stand up on your feet!," which he did. The people reacted as if Paul and Barnabas were Greek gods, and they brought sacrifices to worship them. Paul, of course, strongly denied they were gods and continued preaching about the true God.

But the disbelieving Jews and gentiles from Antioch and Iconium followed them to Lystra and turned the people against Paul and Barnabas. The mob stoned Paul, dragged him outside the city, and left him for dead. But after they left, the disciples gathered around Paul, got him up, and took him back into the city to recover from the attack. The next day Paul and Barnabas continued to travel to the city of Derbe, where they preached and saw many come to faith in Jesus before returning to Antioch to report to the church.

The Questions

1. Were you surprised how quickly those who saw miracles and healings would turn from worshipping Paul and Barnabas to attempting to kill them? What does this reveal about relying on miracles to bring faith?
2. If not miracles, what did Paul rely upon to convince them to put their faith in Jesus?
3. What do you think made the Lystra crowd react with such hostility? Was there something in Paul's message that threatened the beliefs of Lystra or the people from Antioch and Iconium? What threatened them?

The Scripture Memory: Acts 14:21–22

The Hook Questions

If I had been among the crowd in Lystra, how would I have decided whether to worship Jesus or persecute Jesus's followers?

What would most likely influence me now?

NT 12: Church Recognized Salvation by Grace

The Misconceptions

- God's acceptance for salvation is based upon fully obeying Moses's law.
- Non-Jews must observe the Jewish laws and traditions like Jews to be righteous before God.
- The prophets' words in Scripture emphasized that salvation belonged to the Jews and not to the gentiles.

The Passage: Acts 15:1–35

The Main Points

1. Some Jewish believers of Jesus taught circumcision was required for gentiles' salvation.
2. Paul and Barnabas rejected circumcision and were sent to Jerusalem to discuss their belief with the church leadership.
3. Peter believed God's acceptance of gentiles was proven by baptism of the Holy Spirit by grace. James believed Scripture proved gentiles would bear Jesus's name and concluded they should accept gentiles.
4. James concluded they should abstain from food sacrificed to idols, meat from strangled animals, or drinking blood, and they should avoid sexual immorality. These restrictions were written down to be read to the church by Paul, Barnabas, and two other leaders.

The Story

Some Jewish believers from Judah committed to obeying Moses's law came to Antioch to observe Paul and Barnabas's teaching after their first missionary trip among Jews and gentiles. These teachers insisted new gentile believers had to be circumcised for salvation as required by the law of Moses. Paul and Barnabas argued strongly against their beliefs, because God was already saving gentiles without circumcision. The church at Antioch sent Paul and Barnabas to Jerusalem to meet with the highest leaders to resolve their disagreement.

    At Jerusalem, Peter reminded them how the Holy Spirit had come upon the gentiles in Caesarea as the Spirit had first come upon them, and they had agreed God accepted gentiles and purified their hearts by grace. Peter asked, "Why should we place on them the law's demands, which neither we nor our fathers could satisfy? We believe they are saved by the grace of Jesus just as we were."

Then James, the leader of the Jerusalem church, added, "The Scriptures declare that God will take people from the gentiles for himself, so we should not make it difficult for the gentiles who are turning to God." The leaders wrote a letter writing that circumcision would not be required but that gentiles still should not eat food sacrificed to idols or meat that came from strangled animals, or drink blood, or commit sexual immorality.

Paul and Barnabas returned to Antioch, joined by two other leaders from Jerusalem, to gather the church and deliver the letter. The church was very happy with the encouragement they received from the letter. And Paul and Barnabas continued to teach in Antioch.

The Questions

1. Both churches saw this issue as critical to the gospel. What does circumcision represent when compared to the grace of Jesus and the gospel?
2. Why do you think the dietary limitations were important for gentiles to follow with Jewish believers?
3. What did the baptism of the Holy Spirit mean to the Jerusalem church and the church of Antioch?
4. In which ways do you think the Antioch gentiles were encouraged by the Jerusalem church's letter?

The Scripture Memory: Gal 5:6

The Hook Question

Which spiritual practices, other than faith and God's grace alone, do I expect would gain me more righteousness before God?

NT 13: Paul and Silas Freed by an Earthquake

The Misconceptions

- Being persecuted, tortured, or jailed weakens a person's commitment to worship and serve God.
- Doing good for others always results in appreciation.

The Passage: Acts 16:16–40

The Main Points

1. Paul cast out a demon from a slave woman who told the future for money for her owners.
2. When cast out, the owners lost their income and took Paul and Silas to the judge to be beaten and jailed.
3. An earthquake freed them from jail, but they remained in their cell and led the jailer to Jesus.
4. Judge released Paul and Silas without a trial, and they informed him they were Roman citizens illegally jailed.

The Story

Paul wanted to visit the churches he and Barnabas had begun. But Barnabas traveled with Mark to Crete, and Paul continued traveling with Silas.

After visiting the churches, the Holy Spirit directed Paul to go to Macedonia. As they preached in the streets of Philippi, a demon-possessed slave woman who foretold the future for her owners' profit followed them. She pointed out Paul and Silas as servants of God who could explain how to be saved. She followed for several days until Paul grew angry, looked at the woman, and commanded, "In the name of Jesus Christ, come out of her!" The demon came out immediately, but now she no longer brought money to the owners. So the owners dragged Paul and Silas before a judge, charging them with causing a riot and advocating unlawful customs for Romans. The judge ordered Paul and Silas stripped, whipped, and chained in a prison.

At midnight, Paul and Silas were singing hymns in the jail when a violent earthquake caused the doors to fly open and all their chains loosened. Seeing the doors open, the jailer prepared to kill himself, because he was responsible for the prisoners. But Paul and Silas called out to him not to kill himself, because they were alive and had not escaped. The jailer came and fell trembling before them, asking what he must do to be saved. Paul answered, "Believe in the Lord Jesus, and you and your household will be saved." The jailer believed and then washed their wounds and fed them. His house was filled with joy, because they all believed in Jesus.

The next morning, the judge ordered them to be released and to leave peaceably. But they replied they were Roman citizens who had been illegally thrown in jail without a trial. The judge was alarmed, hearing they were Roman citizens, and personally escorted them out of the prison. Paul and Silas went to the new believers in Philippi to encourage them before leaving.

The Questions

1. Why was Paul frustrated with the demon announcing their ministry?
2. Which effects do you think the possessed woman's owners hoped for resulting from the persecution of Paul and Silas by the mob and the judge? Which effects actually happened?
3. Why do you think Paul and Silas didn't interpret the earthquake as God's miracle enabling them to escape? Why did they remain in the jail? How would the story have ended differently if they had escaped?
4. Which reasons might have motivated the judge to release Paul and Silas the next morning without a trial?

The Scripture Memory: 1 Pet 1:6–7; 4:15

The Hook Questions

Would I conclude that the earthquake would be God's miracle to allow me to escape from a jail?

What would I believe was more important than escaping persecution?

NT 14: Paul Debated Greek Philosophy in Athens

The Misconceptions

- Creating temples, idols, and precious objects of worship pleases God and gains his favor.
- There is a god beyond man's knowledge who should be honored as the unknown god.
- God requires and expects people to craft idols and other tokens of worship for him.

The Passage: Acts 17:16–34

The Main Points

1. Paul was persecuted and escaped to Athens, where he debated his message with Greek philosophers.
2. Paul declared Athenians' worship practices of temples and idols were unnecessary, because God created everything in the world, providing everything to satisfy man's needs for life.
3. God desires seekers of him to repent before a future time of judgment by a Judge proven trustworthy by being resurrected from the dead.

The Story

Paul and Silas escaped Philippi for Thessalonica. Though some Thessalonians believed Paul's messages, the unbelievers rioted against the believers, so Paul and Silas escaped to Berea. But the angry Thessalonians followed them to Berea, where the Berean believers sent Paul to Athens alone. Silas and a new companion, Timothy, remained with the new believers, planning to meet Paul later in the city of Corinth. While waiting in Athens, Paul began preaching in the Jewish synagogues, but his news of the resurrection of Jesus was disputed by local Greek philosophers. They argued he was promoting worship of new, foreign gods, so they invited him to a place where philosophies were proposed and debated.

Paul began his message describing how he had seen their many temples and objects made of silver and gold. Some of those objects were dedicated to "the unknown god"; this was the God he wanted to talk about. He began, saying this God created everything in the world, so he doesn't live in temples made by human hands. Because he made everything, he didn't need to be served anything by man. Instead, this is the God who provides life, breath, and everything else man needs, so he himself needs nothing from man.

Because we are this God's offspring, he doesn't need anything made by man for worship but commands man to repent. He has set a date for judgment with justice by a man he appointed, and proved his message by resurrecting this man—Jesus—from the dead. When Paul mentioned the resurrection, some mocked him. But many others followed Paul until he left Athens to sail for Corinth.

The Questions

1. Which value or benefits did the Greeks expect from their gods by building so many temples?
2. What does God want and expect man to offer God who provides all things for man?
3. God has set a future date for judgment. Who will be the judge on that day, and how do we know he will be just?

The Scripture Memory: Acts 7:48–50; 1 Kgs 8:27; Isa 66:1–2

The Hook Question

What does God most expect from me if the sacrificial or devotional objects I've purchased or made are not desired by him and are meaningless to him?

NT 15: Paul Addressed Church Disunity in Corinth

The Misconceptions

- A leader of the church is expected to increase his power, honor, and influence.
- Young believers must place their loyalty and trust in their leaders and teachers.
- Followers should promote their leaders and teachers as superior to all other leaders.

The Passages: Acts 18:1–6; 1 Cor 1:10–15; 3:1–23

The Main Points

1. Paul was protected from harm and taught in Corinth eighteen months before leaving for Ephesus.
2. Paul received reports from Corinth revealing disunity among the believers about following leaders.
3. Paul identified Corinth's problems as immaturity and misunderstanding the united ministry of leaders.

The Story

Paul left Athens for Corinth to be reunited with Silas and Timothy. Paul began teaching in the Jewish synagogues but again met with such opposition that he stopped teaching the Jews and focused on teaching gentiles instead.

One night, God spoke to Paul in a vision telling him not to be afraid of teaching, because God himself would protect him from harm. God also said he had many people in Corinth he wanted Paul to reach. So Paul continued teaching in Corinth for eighteen months before traveling to Ephesus. While at Ephesus, Paul received questions from the Corinthian church and heard reports that the house churches were divided over which leader to follow: Paul, Peter, or Apollos—a teacher from Ephesus. Some believers boasted they followed no man but only Jesus himself!

Paul wrote a letter answering their questions but first addressed the quarreling and jealousy between the house churches. Paul wrote they misunderstood the role of leaders—which was obvious from their jealousy, quarreling, and disunity. They were spiritually immature. Jesus was not divided, Paul was not crucified, and they were all baptized only through the single name of Jesus. Paul and the other leaders were servants through whom they had believed. One leader planted a seed, and another watered it. One planted a foundation on Christ, and another built on top of the foundation. If their building was successful, it would be revealed through time and judgment, because it would last. If their building was unsuccessful, it would be burned up.

Everyone is God's temple, because God's Spirit dwells within. If anyone destroys another's temple, God will destroy that person.

The Questions

1. How can committed loyalty to one leader bring disunity to the larger church community?
2. What can a pastor or leader do to prevent disunity among churches?
3. How should a follower evaluate their teachers and true leaders so they remain focused in their spiritual growth, trust, and understanding?

The Scripture Memory: 1 Pet 5:2

The Hook Questions

Would I prefer to follow a popular leader, a persuasive leader, an educational leader, or a humble servant leader?

How would these choices affect how the church becomes spiritually mature?

NT 16: Paul Taught Faith to Jew and Gentile in Rome

The Misconceptions

- God judges by favoring one people over others.
- God's authority as judge allows him to favor people groups he prefers to love.
- Righteousness results from rigorously obeying the laws of righteousness.

The Passages: Rom 1:13-16; 3:19—4:17

The Main Points

1. Abraham was pronounced righteous before there were any Jews.
2. Abraham was pronounced righteous before the Mosaic law.
3. The law can't make people righteous; the law reveals all people are guilty and accountable of sin.
4. Jesus's sacrifice paid the penalty for all sin, but it is applied to those who seek Christ's righteousness.

The Story

Paul, as a missionary to the gentiles, was often challenged by the Jews who believed they were favored by God because they had received God's laws through Moses. Paul challenged those beliefs with three arguments:

First, Abraham was pronounced righteous before there were Jews who had descended from him.

Second, Abraham was pronounced righteous before the law was given by Moses.

Third, no person can keep the law perfectly.

But these Jews viewed Paul's belief that righteousness did not come from the law as a threat to their national identity. Instead of recognizing their own inability to keep the law perfectly, these Jews boasted about their own righteousness and believed they were favored by God over any other people without God's laws.

Paul argued the law made all people aware of their personal failures and therefore made them accountable for those failures. So the law's purpose was to show all people were guilty, and the law could not declare anyone righteous. All people, whether Jew or gentile, have sinned and are therefore guilty before God.

But, according to the Scriptures, God made another way for righteousness than through the law. As with Abraham, righteousness was given from God through faith in his promised provision. The person who works for his righteousness as an earned wage will not be pronounced a righteous person like Abraham. But the person who believes by faith God's promise of receiving righteousness as a gift, like Abraham will be justified and pronounced righteous.

The Questions

1. How does removing the effort of earning righteousness make salvation accessible to everyone?
2. Why can't anyone boast about their personal righteousness, or their people being favored by God, if righteousness is given as a gift?
3. Which comparisons and expectations of strict religious practices are found in other religions with which you're familiar?

The Scripture Memory: Rom 4:1–3; 5:1–2

The Hook Question

What would motivate me to live righteously if perfect righteousness was already a gift to me through faith in Jesus's perfect sacrifice for me?

NT 17: Paul Affirmed Jesus's Resurrection

The Misconceptions

- There is no resurrection from the dead.
- The body we have on earth is the body that will enter heaven.
- Only a few people saw the ghost of Jesus and not his resurrected body.

The Passages: 1 Cor 15:5–8, 12–58

The Main Points

1. To those denying the resurrection, Paul refers to the many witnesses who saw Jesus resurrected, without which we remain under the penalty of sin, our faith is useless, and we are false witnesses.
2. To those who believe in the resurrection but don't understand it, Paul reminds them that God made different bodies for animals on earth.
3. The human body is weak and sown as seed, being raised in power, splendor, and immortal for heaven.

The Story

Many of the Corinthian citizens denied Jesus was resurrected and actively opposed those who believed In Jesus's resurrection. Paul was no longer in Corinth, and so he wrote a letter to the Corinthian church on how to defend the resurrection against those attacks.

The most important proof was many firsthand witnesses who were available to describe what they saw. There were all of Jesus's disciples, including Peter and James, and more than five hundred people at one time—most of them still alive when Paul, who also had witnessed Jesus's resurrection, wrote the letter.

Second, if Jesus was not resurrected, then all the witnesses were working hard, speaking of things that were not true and useless, because we would all still be under the penalty of death and would all be guilty of bearing false witness.

Other Corinthians believed in the resurrection but wondered how dead bodies would rise. Paul reminded them that God did not make all the bodies on earth the same. Humans have one kind of body, and birds and fish have different bodies. There are earthly bodies for living on earth, but

God made heavenly bodies for living in heaven. The earthly body is the seed for the heavenly body.

All earthly bodies will die and fall into the ground in weakness. But these weak bodies will be raised in power as new, immortal bodies able to live forever in heaven. Earthly flesh and blood must come first and die to be the seed for the heavenly body that lives in heaven without death and to continue the Lord's work. Jesus was resurrected and will return to earth to defeat all kingdoms, authorities, and powers.

The Questions

1. Why does Paul add the detail that most of the over five hundred who saw the resurrected Jesus were still alive?
2. Why can't earthly flesh and blood bodies inherit the kingdom of God?
3. Why should those in the Lord's work be encouraged to continue even though they will die?

The Scripture Memory: John 11:25–26

The Hook Question

Which proof of Jesus's resurrection is most comforting and important to me?

NT 18: Paul Taught Unity by Grace in Ephesus

The Misconceptions

- The Christian gospel is exclusive to Jews only.
- Righteousness and identification of the Messiah come through obedience to Jewish laws and commands.
- Greeks will always be foreigners to Jews and Jesus, because they worshipped idols and foreign gods in their past.

The Passages: Acts 19:8-10; Eph 2:8-17

The Main Points

1. Paul taught Jews in a synagogue for three months before teaching daily in a lecture hall to Jews and gentiles together for two years.
2. Paul taught unity by replacing Jewish laws and commands with grace to receive salvation.
3. The removal of Jewish laws and commands brought Greeks and Jews together into one spiritual temple.

The Story

Whenever Paul arrived in a new city, he usually began teaching the gospel in a Jewish synagogue. Paul did that for three months in Ephesus. But many of the Jews argued so strongly against Paul that he finally left the synagogue and taught daily in a lecture hall for the next two years to both Jews and interested Greeks. He taught the Greeks they were once separate from Jesus without hope or God. They were foreigners to the covenants and commandments God had made with Israel. This made a dividing barrier that prevented Greeks from joining the Jewish believers. This barrier needed to be abolished if there was to be one church for both peoples.

Paul taught that Jesus satisfied all the demands of the law that neither Jew nor Greek could satisfy. Nothing else and no one else could satisfy the law's demands other than the gift of Jesus's perfect sacrifice and blood that could never be earned or paid for by anyone. What Jesus did to remove the law's demands was available only through God's grace, which was available to both Jews and Greeks and broke down the barrier that separated them. Now there could be peace and unity in the one church. The household of

God now fits all believers together with Jesus as the cornerstone and filled by God's presence and the Holy Spirit.

The Questions

1. How does God's grace rather than performing cultural spiritual duties, practices, and laws make the gospel universally accessible to all cultures?
2. What would happen if the gospel was adjusted to personal cultural practices within a multicultural church?
3. How would forcing the loss of personal cultural identity influence the spread of the gospel within the cultural community?

The Scripture Memory: Eph 2:8–9

The Hook Questions

On which side of the dividing wall am I hoping to live: believing in the performance of religious duties or having faith by God's grace alone?

Is fulfilling my current religious demands similar to the barrier of the Jewish law?

NT 19: Paul's Imitators Had No Spiritual Authority

The Misconceptions

- Words alone have spiritual authority to create and control results for either blessings or curses.
- Authoritative power is assumed when speaking the name of God or Jesus.

The Passage: Acts 19:11–20

The Main Points

1. Paul taught in Ephesus for two years and performed miraculous healings.
2. Jewish sorcerers used the names of Jesus and Paul to command demons to leave possessed people.
3. The demons rejected their authority to command them, and the possessed people attacked them.
4. The people feared the word of God, the name of the Lord was honored, and people believed.

The Story

Paul taught in Ephesus for two years and performed many extraordinary, miraculous healings. Some Jews tried to imitate Paul's practices of casting out demons from possessed people by saying, "In the name of Jesus whom Paul preaches, I command you to get out." Seven sons of a Jewish chief priest attempted this imitation, and the demon answered, "Jesus I know, and Paul I know about, but who are you?" Then the possessed man overcame the seven sons and gave them such a beating that they ran out of the house naked and bleeding.

When this became known to the Jews and the Greeks, great fear came upon all the people and the name of Jesus was held in high honor. Many Ephesians confessed their sins and believed in Jesus, and a number of sorcerers brought their magic scrolls and publicly burned them.

The Questions

1. What did the seven sons assume was necessary when they modeled their exorcisms after Paul?
2. Why did the seven sons fail to command the demons to obey them?
3. What is the difference in spiritual power between someone casting an evil eye or spell and what the seven sons said?
4. What is critical in making a command in the name of Jesus?

The Scripture Memory: Matt 7:22–23

The Hook Question

How confident am I that any spiritual authority I have is authentic and can give me spiritual protection?

NT 20: Paul Rejected Using Jewish Law to Mature

The Misconceptions

- We receive salvation by faith but are perfected in righteousness through our efforts.
- The Holy Spirit makes us righteous based upon our obedience to Jewish law.
- Abraham is a blessing only for his own descendants.

The Passages: Gal 3:6–12; 2:11–13; 5:13–23

The Main Points

1. The visiting Jewish Christian believers came to Galatia to require obedience to the law.
2. Paul confronted Peter for following those believers who require obedience to the law.
3. The Scriptures taught that Abraham believed God and his faith caused God to declare him righteous.
4. Faith in God's promises escapes the curse of imperfectly following the law.
5. The Holy Spirit within a believer causes fruitful godliness through the believer's faith.

The Story

Paul wrote a story to the Galatians about confronting the apostle Peter when he visited the church of Antioch. Peter had been eating with the gentile believers until Jewish believers arrived from Jerusalem who insisted that all followers of Jesus had to obey the dietary laws of Moses's law to be righteous. Peter reacted by withdrawing from the gentiles and eating only with the Jerusalem believers. Paul confronted Peter in front of everybody and said, "You are a Jew but you live like a gentile. Why then do you force gentiles to follow Jewish customs? We are not justified by following the laws but by faith in Jesus Christ!"

Paul wanted to teach the Galatians to argue against these legal influencers using Scripture. Paul began by using Abraham's example of believing God's promise, which God honored by declaring Abraham righteous. This declaration promised that both Jews and gentiles who show the same faith as Abraham would also be justified as was Abraham.

Second, the law declared that anyone who relied upon the law to be justified would be cursed unless they kept all the laws perfectly. Those who wanted to add the law's demands to their faith were taking away the freedom found in Jesus by faith!

But how could believers grow spiritually if not by practicing the law perfectly? Paul answered this question by teaching they were called to be free but not to use their freedom to indulge in sin. Instead, they were to fulfill the law by loving and serving others and demonstrating the fruit of the Holy Spirit living within each believer. There are no laws against practicing the fruits of the Spirit!

The Questions

1. Which religious rules or duties, if any, were you taught to follow as a child? Would Paul identify them as laws that measured obedience, purity, improvement, or guilt? How have these rules improved or disappointed your relationship by faith with God?
2. Which righteousness, comfort, or good would you expect to earn if you kept obeying Moses's law perfectly?
3. Do you believe it is possible to obey the law perfectly? Do you know anyone who was perfect?
4. What can a person do to force fruit from a tree? What can you do to either force or encourage fruit from the Holy Spirit?

The Scripture Memory: Gal 5:23

The Hook Questions

Am I more comfortable relying on faith like Abraham or on perfectly fulfilling the requirements of religious practices and duties to be obedient?

What are the strengths and weaknesses of my relying on faith or law?

NT 21: Paul Used Persecution to Glorify God

The Misconceptions

- Persecutions will stop the progress of the church.
- Preaching Jesus will bring only respect and honor.
- Persecution brings discouragement.

The Passages: Phil 1:12–18

The Main Points

1. Paul was in prison for the defense of the gospel.
2. Paul rejoiced in his imprisonment, because the palace guard was hearing about Jesus, and Paul's example encouraged others to tell about Jesus.
3. Paul was encouraged that Jesus was being preached, whether from sincere or insincere motives.

The Story

Paul was in chains, most likely in Rome, when the church at Philippi sent one of their members to provide financial support and encouragement. Paul sent a letter back to them, teaching them about his attitude when being persecuted and imprisoned for preaching about Jesus.

Paul was rejoicing about his imprisonment because more people were learning about Jesus. The Roman palace guard and those who were guarding Paul all heard about Jesus from Paul. And they all knew Paul was imprisoned for the defense of Jesus.

Paul was also rejoicing because Christians were encouraged to speak more courageously and fearlessly in their own situations. Paul knew that some of those preaching were envious of Paul and were ambitious for their own fame and promotion to expand. But others were preaching out of love. To Paul, the motives of both the insincere and the insincere preachers didn't matter, because the greater objective was that people were hearing about Jesus, and for this, Paul was both rejoicing and would continue to rejoice.

Thirty New Testament Story Lessons

The Questions

1. Which honor would a Christian worker expect from ministering to others?
2. Which positive outcomes could God use out of the persecution of Christian workers?
3. Instead of rejoicing in persecution, how may Christians give greater effort toward personal defense and freedom? How would God be glorified in those efforts?

The Scripture Memory: Matt 5:10–11

The Hook Question

How would my closest personal friends react if I rejoiced in persecution for declaring my faith in Jesus?

NT 22: Favoritism Breaks God's Law of Love

The Misconceptions

- Personal clothing choices always accurately reflect people's character.
- The ability to communicate religious convictions indicates a person's religious commitment.
- Personal evaluations and judgments about others don't have a moral context.
- Honor and dignity should be given only to those who have earned it.

The Passage: Jas 2:1–13

The Main Points

1. Offering either honored or dishonored seating based on clothing reveals evil motives of favoritism.
2. The rich and powerful often oppress or dishonor poor people, though God has chosen to bless the poor.
3. Obeying the law to love others as you love yourself prohibits favoritism; allowing favoritism makes a person guilty of breaking the law.

The Story

James, the leader of the first church in Jerusalem, wrote a letter to the younger churches beyond Jerusalem about his concerns and observations. One concern was about favoring one group or individuals over other groups or individuals.

James told a story about two people who entered a congregational gathering. One person was dressed in very fine clothing, and he was directed to a very good place to sit. The other person, however, was dressed in filthy clothing, and he was directed to sit on the floor. James suspected those who directed the seating used questionable and evil motives to influence their directions where to seat them. Why did they direct those who appeared rich and powerful to more favorable seating, even though it was often the rich and powerful who oppressed or dishonored the poor? Hadn't God chosen the poor of the world to be rich in faith to inherit God's kingdom promised to them?

James warned them that showing favoritism of one over another was violating God's command to love their neighbors as they loved themselves. Showing favoritism breaks God's command to love, and judgment will be merciless to those who have shown no mercy, because mercy always triumphs over judgment.

The Questions

1. Which behavior have you observed in a church gathering that revealed favoritism of one over another?
2. Should those who are poor and don't contribute anything to the community still be honored? Why or why not?
3. What is the basis for granting honor and dignity to others?

The Scripture Memory: Jas 2:8

The Hook Questions

Which common customs and practices does my culture value and respect?

If I choose to withhold my respect from anyone who doesn't reflect my social status or honor, should I also withhold my love from them?

How could I still show love to them and give my honor to someone loved by God?

NT 23: Hope Overcomes Shame and Persecution

The Misconceptions

- God protects those who believe in Jesus from experiencing shame and mistreatment.
- Retaliation is the best way to protect honor when falsely accused, shamed, or abused.
- The shame of dishonor has no positive benefit.

The Passages: 1 Pet 1:6–7; 2:12–23

The Main Points

1. Peter wrote to encourage believers who were being maligned and slandered for their faith.
2. First, hope in proven faith that will be honored by Jesus at his return.
3. Second, look to Jesus as the model who never retaliated against his accusers.
4. Third, persecution is not unfair if it is deserved punishment for evil works.

The Story

Following Jesus's death, Peter began leading the disciples and preaching about Jesus. Peter was often put in prisons and often beaten. But he continued to form small churches for those who believed his message. And those who became believers were also maligned, slandered, and put to shame in their towns and villages, so the new believers would return to their own majority practices and beliefs.

From his own experience, Peter knew the encouragement they needed, and he sent a letter to circulate among the churches. He shared three important principles. First was hope that, though they were distressed by these trials, the proof of their faith would result in praise, glory, and honor when Jesus Christ returned. Second, they were to look at Jesus as their model who didn't retaliate with the same anger as he faced or make threats against those who shamed him. And third, they were to make certain that if they were being slandered, it was for their good works and the honor of Jesus and not because of deserved wrongs or evil.

The Questions

1. What do you think Peter placed his hope upon despite being shamed and beaten for Jesus?
2. Why do people shame others and others retaliate with shame? What makes shame successful or unsuccessful?
3. Do you think Jesus would have been successful if he had retaliated against those mocking him? Why or why not?

The Scripture Memory: 1 Pet 4:12-13

The Hook Question

Why should I continue to tell others about Jesus even if I am persecuted for doing it?

NT 24: From Resurrection to the Kingdom

The Misconceptions

- The resurrection of Jesus reveals the successful completion of Jesus's mission.
- The resurrection of Jesus was a disproved hoax.
- The resurrection of Jesus emphasizes Jesus but not his followers.

The Passages: 1 Cor 15:5–13, 20–28

The Main Points

1. Denial of resurrection issue was answered by witnesses.
2. Resurrection of followers is necessary for the kingdom.
3. Jesus subjects all rule, authority, and power to present kingdom to the Father.

The Story

Some of the Corinthians said there was no resurrection of the dead. Paul argued in a letter to them that if there was no resurrection of the dead, then Jesus has not been raised. However, Jesus was seen by many witnesses, and he ate food with Him. And Jesus's resurrection from the dead was the firstfruits of believers who will also be raised from the dead for the mission that remains to be accomplished.

Jesus did not return to the same existence he had before he died, but he was first to be resurrected before any of his believers would follow him in to heaven with a new body fit for a heavenly existence. But the resurrection was not the end of Jesus's work, because Jesus still had to abolish all remaining rule, authority, and power against him and then finally defeat the last enemy, death. After that, Jesus will hand over the kingdom and himself to the Father.

Those who deny the resurrection do not recognize that Jesus—and his followers—is still at work until the kingdom is handed to the Father from the Son.

The Questions

1. What is the relationship between the resurrection and the coming kingdom?
2. What should Jesus and his followers be doing during these present days until God's kingdom comes?
3. If death represents the limitations that end life and all things, what does the defeat of death mean to believers of the arrival of the new kingdom?
4. How would believing in the hope of a resurrected body conquer any fears of death or dying?

The Scripture Memory: 1 Cor 15:42–44

The Hook Question

How does understanding the work Jesus is continuing to do to bring me into the completed kingdom of God the Father change my expectation of what I'll be doing in heaven?

NT 25: God Uses the Weak and Humble

The Misconceptions

- Trust the wisdom of those who are powerful and influential to guide your life decisions.
- Trust Jewish history and spiritual signs to guide your decisions.
- Those who are weak and despised have no value or influence on others.
- Wealth and power indicate God's blessing.

The Passage: 1 Cor 1:18–31

The Main Points

1. The Jews look for signs, and the Greeks look for wisdom presented by influential and wealthy people.
2. God chose the crucifixion of Jesus, which appeared foolish to the Greeks and unexplainable to the Jews.
3. God rejects those Greek and Jewish influential leaders who seek to disprove the crucifixion but accepts the weak and despised who, instead, point others to the crucified Christ for righteousness, sanctification, and redemption.

The Story

Paul wanted to teach the church in Corinth why his message about Jesus was attacked so differently by the Jews and by the Greeks. Paul explained that Jews looked for spiritual signs to disprove the story of Jesus's crucifixion and the resurrection, but the Greeks looked for wisdom from influential political leaders and their Greek social nobility to disprove the story of Jesus. Paul said either approach would fail, because the wisdom of man could not come to know God and the crucifixion was a stumbling block to the Jews.

Instead, God chose to use the preaching of the crucifixion to shame the wise, and the weak things of the world to shame the strong things. It would be through preaching about Jesus that those who were called by God—both Jews and Greeks—would believe.

Paul told them to look around at those in their church whom God had called to believe and realize that most were not from influential families or political leaders. Instead, whom has God been calling? God has preferred to call many who were weak or despised to be filled with the Holy Spirit instead of those who were great in the world's eyes. According to Paul, this is so that no one boasts in their own greatness but boasts only in the Lord for their righteousness, sanctification, and redemption.

The Questions

1. Why does God want to destroy the Greeks' dependence on wisdom?
2. Why doesn't God depend upon the influence of social leaders or politics to build his church?
3. Why does God value those who are weak and humble to testify about Jesus's crucifixion and resurrection?

The Scripture Memory: 1 Cor 1:30

The Hook Questions

Which weaknesses do I think I have?

How could God use those weaknesses for me to influence others?

Why would God want to use my weaknesses for his glory?

NT 26: Serving Others Using Different Gifts

The Misconceptions

- Those with public gifts should likewise be publicly honored.
- Those who only want to quietly serve others make their own decisions when to serve.
- Believers can identify their own gifts according to their own desires.
- Believers choose when to use, how to use, and when to limit the use of their gifts.

The Passage: Rom 12:3–8

The Main Points

1. Personal decision to join Christian gatherings
2. Gifts distributed by the Holy Spirit to serve others.
3. Everyone has a unique gift to contribute, like the parts that make up the body.

The Story

The first gatherings of Roman believers met in homes. These believers all had different gifts—some were spiritually gifted, and others had special talents and skills. But all could be used to serve others in their homes, because all individual members were members of one spiritual body.

Paul saw how some of the people elevated the importance of some gifts over others, and some became prideful about their gifts. Others didn't consider their gifts to be as important as others' gifts and didn't practice using their gifts.

Paul wrote to these Roman house churches that all their gifts were given by the Holy Spirit and were to be used to the extent of their faith, whether in preaching, serving, or teaching. Those gifted in leadership were to be diligent in leading and showing mercy with cheerfulness.

Paul wanted all the believers to love one another and to be devoted to others in their service to each other, being an encouragement and liberally contributing to help others and offering hospitality.

The Questions
- How would a person identify their spiritual gift?
- Why is it good that the Holy Spirit distributes his gifts by faith and not according to anyone's own preference?
- Why should believers never be prideful about their spiritual gifts?

The Scripture Memory: Rom 12:5

The Hook Questions

Among those who know me best, whom should I ask to help me honestly know which spiritual gifts I may have?

How should I develop those gifts?

NT 27: The Indwelling Spirit Gives Power over Sin

The Misconceptions

- Anyone can resist temptation and sin empowered by their own will.
- There is no evidence that people are too spiritually weak to resist sin.
- Those who rely on their own power are able to defeat spiritual temptations or attacks.

The Passage: Rom 7:17—8:11

The Main Points

1. Paul desired to do good but did not, and he desired to avoid evil but did not.
2. Sin dwelt within Paul and enslaved him.
3. Paul needed power over his indwelling sin. When sin is forgiven, the needed power comes from the Spirit of God and empowers Paul.

The Story

The apostle Paul was frustrated. He wanted to serve, obey God, and do good things, but he often failed to do such things. And he didn't want to do evil things he hated, but those were the things he did. Why could he stop doing the good he desired but couldn't stop doing the evil he wanted to avoid? Why couldn't he carry out the good and stop doing the evil?

Paul concluded that it was the sin nature that dwelled within him and within all people. This was the source that could overcome his desire to do good things and encourage him to do evil instead. This was what made him a slave to evil. What could give him the power to overcome this slavery of sin, because he had no power within himself to do that?

But what Paul recognized was that both the source of this power and the power itself were outside of himself. It was Jesus's death on the cross as a sin offering that, by faith, allowed Paul to apply that offering for himself. With his sin forgiven, the Spirit of God—the source of the power—would dwell within him and cause the body to become dead to sin's power and strengthened in righteousness! The power of the indwelling Spirt of God is accessible to the person who will live, because those who are led by the Spirit are sons of God!

The Questions

1. What is the source of evil, which indwells every person?
2. If Paul does not have the power within him to resist evil, where must the power come from to strengthen him to do what is good and to resist evil?
3. What would qualify and encourage the Spirit of God to dwell within any person?

The Scripture Memory: Rom 8:9

The Hook Question

What are the despairing evil habits or actions that I feel limit my spiritual growth and attack my spiritual weaknesses?

NT 28: God Controls All Things to Guarantee Hope

The Misconceptions

- A hope and a wish are the same thing.
- No one can fulfill a promise, because future events are unknown and uncontrolled.
- Nothing can protect everyone from persecution.

The Passages: 1 Pet 1:3–13, 21

The Main Points

1. Persecution caused concern about dying and not receiving eternal life.
2. Two assurances of hope—Jesus's resurrection and inheritance of eternal life—are protected by God.
3. Hope of eternal life brings confidence to survive through persecution.

The Story

The early church was experiencing persecution from both the Roman emperor Nero and the local people who objected to the message of Jesus. The churches were uncertain they could survive the persecutions in their own abilities and strengths. The apostle Peter felt responsible for them and wrote a letter of encouragement to them. Peter wrote about two assurances for their hope of eternal life.

The first assurance was that Jesus's own resurrection from the dead provided the model for them to be born again to a living hope. The second assurance was knowing their inheritance of eternal life was reserved in heaven for each of them; could not fade away or be defiled; and was protected by the power of God through their faith.

These two assurances of a living hope of eternal life and that it is reserved in heaven and protected by God himself removes all fears and concerns during persecution and enduring trials. This hope from God is not simply a wish that may not be fulfilled because of dangerous changes in future conditions but a hope from God who controls all conditions and situations that could affect the fulfillment of eternal life. The hope of eternal life will be fulfilled by God.

The Questions

1. Have you ever made a promise you couldn't keep because of changes you couldn't control?
2. What makes God's promises impossible not to fulfill?
3. How would knowing you had eternal life that had been promised by God affect your decisions and fears?

The Scripture Memory: 1 Pet 1:3

The Hook Questions

Is eternal life something I hope for or something I'm not convinced exists?

When the Bible speaks about eternal life, is it unconditionally promised, or is it dependent on future events beyond my control?

NT 29: Forgiveness Restores Fellowship with God

The Misconceptions

- Keeping in fellowship with God requires staying perfectly sinless.
- Confessing sins means making a list to name them all.
- Being guilty of sin removes the ability to be restored to walk in God's light again.

The Passage: 1 John 1:5–10

The Main Points

1. Being obedient to God's commands brings us into God's light for fellowship.
2. No one can remain in God's light by being sinless, because all people sin.
3. Confession (agreement on what is sin) allows for forgiveness, God's cleansing, and restoration to God's light and fellowship.

The Story

As the young believers formed a new church under the leadership of the apostle John, they were taught to obey the commands of Jesus. John taught that praying and being obedient to God's commands would keep them walking by God's light. They would be clean and walking in God's light and remaining in fellowship together.

Over time, some believed they could maintain constant obedience; they were sinless and always remained spiritually clean. Others believed they had failed and were in danger of losing their fellowship with God. They wondered what they had to do to have their sins forgiven once again to be restored to God's light.

So John wrote a letter to them, writing that both views were wrong. To those who believed they were sinless, he wrote they were not truthful with themselves and were calling God a liar, because God had said all people have sin. And for those who became aware and ashamed of their sinful thoughts or actions, God promised that if they confessed their sin—which is a word that means agreement with God's evaluation that some actions, lack of actions, and thoughts are, in fact, sin—then God would forgive them and cleanse them from their shame and unrighteousness.

Thirty New Testament Story Lessons

The Questions

1. Why are persons who believe they are sinless an insult to God?
2. How do believers who constantly mourn and show great humility and sadness over their sin reject God's promise and his cleansing?
3. How does being forgiven over and over again for confessed sin affect your appreciation for Jesus's sacrifice and for God's desire that we fellowship in God's light?

The Scripture Memory: 1 John 1:9

The Hook Questions

When have I felt so ashamed of a sin I repeated often that I couldn't pray or do my religious duties, and so I tried to hide from God like Adam and Eve did in the garden?

But do I believe that God will chase me down, so I finally will ask for forgiveness and receive God's cleansing and live in the light?

NT 30: Satan's Works and Jesus's Glory Revealed

The Misconceptions

- Symbolic language is used to describe "real-world" items in detail.
- Evil purposes are not repetitive or universal across time and location.
- Understanding the historic, constant presence of good and evil in the world enables believers to know how to accept and relate to evil.

The Passage: Rev 4–22

The Main Points

1. Disobedience of God has always been present since Gen 3.
2. The prostitute and the beast are symbols of evil empires.
3. The new Jerusalem and life-giving water are used as symbols of goodness.
4. God, not man, will judge and bring vengeance like a winepress to those who choose evil.

The Story

Sometimes, God revealed information to his prophets, kings, and godly leaders through dreams or visions. The apostle John was imprisoned on an island when he received a lengthy vision revealing how the conflict between good and evil appears throughout history and until the end-time when Jesus presents the kingdom to the Father.

God used symbols to teach John about Satan's rebellion against God's rule throughout history and into the future. For example, the evil empires of both Rome and Babylon are historical but also representative of evil empires in the future. These empires are represented as a prostitute, because they use people for their own desires and power and economically drain other countries, and as a beast to represent military-political power and political religions.

God also revealed to John a new Jerusalem coming down from heaven to establish God's kingdom on earth. The prostitute was described as drunk with wine, which compares with the new Jerusalem offering the water of life. Symbols of blessing first found in the creation story of Gen 1–2 reappear as the new Jerusalem descends to earth to bring those blessings once again.

God judges those who support the beast, including Satan, and the description of judgment uses the Old Testament picture of a winepress for those who fight against God's kingdom. Satan is sent to hell, but as the new Jerusalem descends from heaven, it is populated by believers cleansed by Jesus's sacrifice. God alone is the judge of the nonbelievers who fight against God.

The Questions

1. Which care should be given when trying to interpret word pictures as symbols?
2. Why do you think the new Jerusalem won't be the same as the present-day Jerusalem?
3. Why aren't the believing followers of God, cleansed by Jesus, also fighting against Satan and his followers in judgment? What does that reveal about how present-day followers should respond to persecutors and unbelievers?
4. How does this revelation of good, evil, and judgment help us interpret and properly respond to the events and leaders of this present age?

The Scripture Memory: Rev 22:13–14

The Hook Question

Do I fear the coming day of the winepress, or do I welcome the day that I will be delivered from the final judgment and welcomed into the new Jerusalem with the new water and the return of the tree of life?

www.ingramcontent.com/pod-product-compliance
Lightning Source LLC
Chambersburg PA
CBHW070318230426
43663CB00011B/2171